Philosophy for Everyone

'*Philosophy for Everyone* is an accessible introduction to some of the most fundamental topics in philosophy with a contemporary twist. It exemplifies the virtues of treating philosophy as an activity that anyone can engage in.'

Michael P. Lynch, *University of Connecticut, USA*

Philosophy for Everyone begins by explaining what philosophy is before exploring the questions and issues at the foundation of this important subject.

Key topics and their areas of focus include:

- Epistemology – what our knowledge of the world and ourselves consists in, and how we come to have it;
- Philosophy of science – foundational conceptual issues in scientific research and practice;
- Philosophy of mind – what it means for something to have a mind, and how minds should be understood and explained;
- Moral philosophy – the nature of our moral judgments and reactions, whether they aim at some objective moral truth, or are mere personal or cultural preferences; and
- Metaphysics – fundamental conceptual questions about the nature of reality.

Designed to be used on the corresponding Introduction to Philosophy online course offered by the University of Edinburgh, this book is also highly recommended for anyone looking for a short overview of this fascinating discipline.

Matthew Chrisman, Duncan Pritchard, Jane Suilin Lavelle, Michela Massimi, Alasdair Richmond and **Dave Ward** are all members of the School of Philosophy, Psychology and Language Sciences at the University of Edinburgh, UK.

Philosophy for Everyone

**Edited by
Matthew Chrisman and Duncan
Pritchard**

**Jane Suilin Lavelle
Michela Massimi
Alasdair Richmond
Dave Ward**

Routledge
Taylor & Francis Group

LONDON AND NEW YORK

Introduction to Philosophy: Online Course

 THE UNIVERSITY of EDINBURGH

Taught by Dr. Dave Ward, Professor Duncan Pritchard, Dr. Michela Massimi, Dr. Suilin Lavelle, Dr. Matthew Chrisman, Dr. Allan Hazlett and Dr. Alasdair Richmond

This completely free and open online course will introduce you to some of the main areas of contemporary philosophy. Each week a different philosopher will talk you through some of the most important questions and issues in their area of expertise. We'll begin by trying to understand what philosophy is – what are its characteristic aims and methods, and how does it differ from other subjects? Then we'll spend the rest of the course gaining an introductory overview of several different areas of philosophy. Topics you'll learn about will include:

- Epistemology, where we'll consider what our knowledge of the world and ourselves consists in, and how we come to have it;
- Philosophy of science, where we'll investigate foundational conceptual issues in scientific research and practice;
- Philosophy of Mind, where we'll ask questions about what it means for something to have a mind, and how minds should be understood and explained;
- Moral Philosophy, where we'll attempt to understand the nature of our moral judgements and reactions – whether they aim at some objective moral truth, or are mere personal or cultural preferences, and;
- Metaphysics, where we'll think through some fundamental conceptual questions about the nature of reality.

Watch an intro video and signup for the course at www.coursera.org/course/introphil.

This edition published 2014
By Routledge
2 Park Square, Milton Park, Abingdon, Oxon, OX14 4RN

Simultaneously published in the USA and Canada
by Routledge
711 Third Ave., New York City, NY 10017

Routledge is an imprint of the Taylor & Francis Group, an informa business

© 2013 Matthew Chrisman, Duncan Pritchard, with Dave Ward,
Jane Suilin Lavelle, Michela Massimi, and Alasdair Richmond

The right of the editors to be identified as the authors of the
editorial material, and of the authors for their individual chapters,
has been asserted in accordance with sections 77 and 78 of the
Copyright, Designs and Patents Act 1988.

British Library Cataloguing in Publication Data
A catalogue record for this book is available from the British
Library

Library of Congress Cataloging in Publication Data
Philosophy for everyone / edited by Matthew Chrisman and Duncan
Pritchard, with Dave Ward, Jane Suilin Lavelle, Michela Massimi, and
Alasdair Richmond.
pages cm
Includes bibliographical references and index.
1. Philosophy–Textbooks. I. Chrisman, Matthew. II. Pritchard, Duncan.
BD31.P565 2013
100–dc23
2013022181

ISBN: 978-0-415-71945-2 (hbk)
ISBN: 978-0-415-71947-6 (pbk)
ISBN: 978-1-315-85788-6 (ebk)

Typeset in Times
by Taylor & Francis Books

Contents

Preface

Have you ever wondered what knowledge is, or whether we have any? What about whether morality is objective or subjective? Or have you thought about what makes the difference between beings with minds like ourselves and things that don't (seem to) have minds, like bicycles or computers? Should we trust what other people say, especially if they report spectacular occurrences; and if so, why? What about the question of whether scientific theories aim to be true or merely to capture the observable data in an attractive way? Do you think time travel is possible; and if you do, what does that mean for the nature of time?

These are philosophical questions. As the American philosopher Wilfrid Sellars once wrote, 'to achieve success in philosophy would be … to "know one's way around" with respect to all these things, not in that unreflective way in which the centipede of the story knew its way around before it faced the question, "how do I walk?", but in that reflective way which means that no intellectual holds are barred.' The aim of this book is to introduce you to the way philosophers think about such questions. That is, we hope to unbar the intellectual holds and help you to begin to think reflectively about issues that we all already, in some implicit and unreflective sense, know our way around.

We start in Chapter 1 with a general introduction to the practice of philosophy. Here you'll find out a bit more about philosophical questions, and what makes them philosophical. You'll also learn about the way philosophers typically go about trying to address such questions in a careful and systematic way. In Chapter 2 we turn to an area of philosophy known as epistemology. Here we ponder questions about the nature of knowledge and whether we even have any knowledge. Next, in Chapter 3 we explore some central issues in the philosophy of mind, most importantly what a mind is. In Chapter 4 we consider another branch of philosophy: ethical theory. We'll consider several important views about the status of morality, whether it is objective, personally or culturally relative, or emotive. After that, we turn in Chapter 5 to an issue in the history of philosophy: the debate between David Hume and Thomas Reid about whether and when we should trust the testimony of others. The philosophy of science is next in Chapter 6. Here we explore the question of the nature and aims of science: is its ambition to get the true theory of how reality is or just to construct an empirically adequate model of observable phenomena? Finally, we turn in Chapter 7 to an important issue in the branch of philosophy called metaphysics: the possibility of time travel. This is not only interesting to fans of science fiction but also to philosophers concerned with the nature of time and other aspects of reality.

Each chapter is followed by a brief summary, some study questions, and a list of further readings and internet resources. In each chapter, key terms are emphasized in bold when they're first used. If a word is emphasized in this way, you can review its definition in the glossary that you'll find at the end of the book.

This scramble through various parts of philosophy is not intended to be a comprehensive introduction to the subject (for that we'd need a much longer book). Rather it's intended to introduce just some of the interesting topics philosophers think about and to illustrate their way of thinking about these topics so that it is accessible to an intelligent reader who has not previously studied philosophy but who is willing to read carefully and think deeply. If you, the reader, have made it this far, we're fully confident you fit the bill. Welcome to the team!

Although we mean for the book to be useable as a general introduction for everyone to philosophy (hence the name), this book was born out of a 'MOOC' offered through the University of Edinburgh. A MOOC is a free and open-source 'massive open online course'. Our MOOC initially ran in the spring of 2013 with seven video lectures, a lively discussion board, and self- and peer-assessments online. We'd like to thank our colleague Dave Ward for spearheading the effort in our Philosophy Department to put together the course and for writing Chapter 1. We'd like to thank our other MOOChers who contributed to this volume: Jane Suilin Lavelle, Michela Massimi and Alasdair Richmond. And we'd like to thank the University of Edinburgh for institutional support, especially Jeff Haywood, Amy Woodgate and Lucy Kendra. Our intention is to repeat and refine the course in the future. So, you may be reading this book because you are enrolled in one of the future instalments of our MOOC. But if you've come to the book in some other way, you might be interested in enrolling in the next instalment of our MOOC. Check us out online.

Matthew Chrisman
Duncan Pritchard

1 What is philosophy?

Dave Ward

Introduction

What is philosophy? I once asked this question of a group of students who had just begun studying at the University of Edinburgh. After a thoughtful pause, one of the group suggested, 'There ain't nothing to it but to do it.' Now, taken by itself this answer is, perhaps, not terribly informative. But nonetheless I think it's importantly right. Philosophy, as we'll see in this chapter and in this book, is an *activity*. And so to find out what it's all about we need to do more than just try to describe it – what I'll attempt to do in this chapter – we need to get stuck in and *do it*. So, if you want to find out what philosophy is, the best thing to do is to work your way through the book in your hands. By doing so you'll get a good idea of the sorts of questions philosophers ask, both today and throughout history, and of the distinctive ways they try to answer them. More importantly, if this book does its job, you should find yourself actively engaging with those questions – puzzling over them, articulating your own thoughts about them, and considering how you might defend those thoughts in response to those who don't agree with you.

So, philosophy is an activity, and you'll find examples of, and invitations to, this activity within the pages of this book. What else can we say about it? The goal of this chapter is to see if we can characterize philosophy in more detail. I'm going to suggest that philosophy is *the activity of working out the right way to think about things*. In the rest of this chapter I'll try to say a bit more about what this means, and why I think it's right. We'll start by thinking about how this characterization of philosophy relates it to other subjects. Then we'll note some features of philosophy that follow from this characterization of it, and consider how philosophers go about looking for 'the right way to think about things'. And finally we'll consider why philosophy, as I describe it in this chapter, might be an interesting or important thing to do.

Stepping back: philosophy and other subjects

Philosophy, I've just claimed, is the activity of working out the right way to think about things. But don't people in all subjects – from astronomy to zoology – try to think about things in the right way? What makes philosophy different from these, or any other, subjects? To see what makes philosophy different, we need to distinguish between what we do when we *step back and work out the right way* to think about something and what we do when we get on with *actually thinking about something* in whatever way we've decided (or perhaps just uncritically accepted) is the right one. We can see this distinction, between working out the right way of thinking and getting on with thinking in that way, as corresponding to the distinction between *doing some academic subject* (lets take physics as our example for now) and *doing philosophy about that subject*. So, when we're doing physics we might be interested in constructing experiments, recording data, and trying to use that data to construct a theory that adequately explains all the data that we've observed, and hopefully all the data we ever will observe. When we're doing this, let's suppose (with due apologies to physicists for my crude characterization of what they get up to), we're engaged in the sort of thinking that's characteristic of physics. However, we can always *step back*, and ask whether this way of thinking is the right one. We can ask what it is for data to confirm or refute a theory; we can ask what it is for one theory to do a better or worse job of explaining some data than another; we can even ask whether the project of trying to explain and understand physical reality by identifying fundamental constituents and processes, and laws that govern them, is the right one. When we step back in this way we shift from asking questions about physics to asking questions within *the philosophy of physics* – from getting on with the way of thinking that physics recommends to working out whether (or why) that way of thinking is the right one. You'll have the opportunity to think about such questions in the philosophy of science in more detail in Chapter 6.

Let's take one more example to illustrate this distinction between actually doing some subject and doing the *philosophy of* that subject. Suppose we are medieval medics, trying to understand some disease. In keeping with the medical understanding of our time, we'll try to understand the disease in terms of the four 'humours' – blood, yellow bile, black bile and phlegm – that we believe fill the human body, and whose imbalance we believe to be the cause of all disease. Our theorizing about the disease might take the form of identifying its symptoms, and then attempting to relate them to the characteristics we associate with some one of the four humours, so we can understand the disease as a lack or a surplus of that humour. In doing this, as the good medieval medics that we are, we're simply getting on with the practice of medical theory. However, we can always step back and ask *further* questions about the framework and presuppositions underlying this theory: we can ask what, exactly, it is for the humours to be in or out of balance; we can ask how, exactly, the humours relate to the types of temperament and personality with which they're supposed to be paired; and (most importantly) we can ask whether we are thinking about human disease and treatment in the right way at all – whether we might be better off stepping outside of the framework of humour theory completely, and trying to find a different one. Using the example of medieval medicine makes it clear that stepping back in this way is often an important thing to do – questioning this theoretical framework and trying to replace it with a better one has resulted in great advances in how we diagnose and treat diseases. But note that I could equally have used *modern* medicine as an example. It seems that in *any* field we can always step back from the task of getting on with our inquiry, try to get a clear view of the framework or set of presuppositions that shapes our inquiry, and question whether that framework is the best one for the job.

So, in both the above examples, physics and (medieval) medicine, we can distinguish between (i) getting on with thinking or investigating according to the rules, practices and assumptions of some theoretical discipline, and (ii) stepping back to investigate just what those rules, practices and assumptions are, and thinking about whether they are the right ones. Stepping back in this way – attempting to identify, clarify and assess the presuppositions that lie behind how we're thinking or acting – is what we do when we engage in philosophy. Thinking about philosophy in this way lets us see a number of important things about it.

First, the boundaries between philosophy and other subjects can be fuzzy. Our second example above raised the question of how we might move from a framework that we now view as outdated and inadequate (such as the humour theory in medicine) to a better one. One way we might do so is simply by thinking about it – when we talk about humours, do we really know what we mean? When we try to think of some disease as a lack of phlegm, or a surplus of bile, do we really have a good grip on what it would mean for a disease to *be* one of those things? This way of trying to identify and assess the concepts and categories we're using 'from our armchairs' is one way we can attempt to work out the right way to think about things. So this kind of armchair theorizing about the concepts we use and the work that we do is one way of doing philosophy – perhaps the way that people most commonly think of as doing philosophy. But this isn't the only way we can try to find the right way to think about things. We might come to revise the way we're thinking about medicine as a result of getting out of our armchairs and actually trying to do it – we might, for example, notice that our humour theory suggests that certain ways of treating diseases should work, but in reality they simply don't. Or we might notice that some other ways of treating diseases, that don't seem to have anything to do with humours or their balance, work really well. If we come across enough observations like this, and if the observations form a neat and obvious enough pattern, then this too can prompt us to start thinking about medicine in another way. We might put this by saying that challenges to our way of thinking can either come from *inside,* as in cases when we realize that the framework we're using to think about things is unstable or confused *just by thinking about it,* or from *outside,* as when the puzzles and unexplained events with which the world confronts our current way of thinking become so widespread that we're forced to look for a new framework that makes better sense of things. We noted above that to challenge ways of thinking 'from the inside' (or 'from the armchair') is something characteristically associated with philosophy. So we can do philosophy of anthropology, biology, chemistry or zoology by trying to identify the frameworks that those subjects use to think about the world, and considering whether those frameworks involve any confusions or contradictions that we might identify and try to resolve. But in many cases (and this is where the lines between philosophy and other subjects get blurry) when we're working out how best to revise our ways of thinking in light of the puzzles that the world has thrown up for us, we're also doing philosophy.

Returning to the example of physics, think of what happened in the early twentieth century with the development of quantum mechanics. There was a growing body of data that, it seemed, simply couldn't be made sense of by using the current ways of thinking about physical reality. It appeared, for example, that the natural assumption that the elements of reality must behave *either* like waves *or* like particles (but not both) might be wrong. And it seemed that the very act of observing or measuring some physical quantity could instantly change how things were in some other part of the universe – apparently violating our common-sense conception of how causation works. Now, clearly the project of working out the best way to think about all these results, and their implications for our understanding of reality, wasn't a purely philosophical one. After all, we needed science to provide and describe the strange experimental results that posed the challenge to our current ways of thinking in the first place. And, in some cases, we needed to seek out new experimental results to test whether our attempted revisions to our thinking were on the right track. Nonetheless, in attempting to revise our ways of thinking in light of results from quantum mechanics we are still doing philosophy. We're stepping back from the results in question and trying to arrive at a new framework that can make the best sense of them.

For example, do we need to change how we think about what it is for one thing to cause another so that we can make sense of causation that happens at a distance? Or do these results show us that trying to use a common-sense notion of causation in our understanding of the nature of microphysical reality is simply misguided? In either case, is there a new and better way of thinking that we can employ to help us get our heads round these strange results? As just noted, whatever new framework we come up with will be informed by work done by scientists, not by philosophers, and many of the tests we'll use to determine whether it is a *good* framework will also involve scientists formulating and experimentally testing the predictions it makes. But in actually coming up with that framework we're stepping back from the process of getting those results, and trying to work out the best way of thinking about them – the activity that I'm suggesting is characteristic of philosophy. Here, as in many places, the relationship between the findings that provide us with food for thought, and the subsequent thinking that feeds off them, is a close and intricate one – and it's this kind of relationship that can make the boundaries between philosophy and other subjects blurry.

Philosophy: difficult, important and everywhere

These points about the relationship between philosophy and other subjects point us towards some other important features of philosophy. They show us, for example, that philosophy is a very broad subject. It seems that no matter what subject matter we're investigating, or how we're investigating it, we can always step back, try to identify the presuppositions that inform our investigation, and think about whether they're the best ones. In the examples above, we saw how stepping back can take us from doing physics, or medicine, to doing *philosophy of* physics or of medicine. And it seems that we can step back in a similar way no matter what subject we're studying, or how we're studying it. This means that, whatever we're doing, a philosophical question – a question about whether the framework we're using is the best one for the job – is never far away.

Think about the kind of exchange that the comedian Louis CK reports having with his daughter (lightly edited here to remove some colourful language):

> You can't answer a kid's question – a kid never accepts any answer! A kid never goes 'Oh, thanks, I get it', they just keep coming with more questions: 'Why? Why? Why?' ... this goes on for *hours and hours*, and at the end it gets so weird and abstract, and at the end it's like: 'Why?'
> 'Well, because some things *are*, and some things *are not*.'
> ' ... Why?'
> [*annoyed*] 'Well because things that *are not* can't *be!*'
> 'Why?'
> 'BECAUSE THEN NOTHING WOULDN'T BE! You can't have ... *nothing isn't! Everything is!!*'
> 'Why?'
> 'Because if nothing wasn't, there'd be all kinds of stuff that we don't ... like giant ants walking around with top hats, dancing around! There's no room for all that stuff!'
> 'Why?'
> [Louis gives up.]
> (Louis CK's 2005 HBO Special 'One Night Stand')

What's happening in this dialogue shows us something about what happens in philosophy. The philosopher is a lot like the daughter in the conversation – continually demanding reasons and explanations for why we think and act in the ways we do. But they also have to do Louis's job – struggling to come up with answers to questions like these, a struggle that sometimes involves trying to explain why they're the wrong questions to be asking. This illustrates a number of important points about philosophy.

First – the one we've just noted – if we keep questioning we soon run into questions that look philosophical: above, Louis quickly gets into some deep metaphysical water over questions about existence (you'll have the opportunity to think more about issues in **metaphysics** in Chapters 6 and 7).

Second, *philosophy is hard.* Being incessantly confronted with questions by children, or by philosophers, presumably wouldn't be such a frustrating experience if we had easy answers at the ready for each question posed to us.

Third (and closely related to the last point), it seems that philosophy is often hard precisely *because* it asks questions about things that we usually take for granted while we get on with our lives. Presumably part of what's frustrating about struggling to answer questions like the ones being put to Louis is that questions like 'Why doesn't everything exist?' can seem so basic as to not require answering. '*Of course* there are things that don't exist', we want to say: this seems so obvious to us that the question strikes us as a silly one to ask. But when it *is* asked, we find ourselves struggling to provide reasons for our convictions that can satisfy the questioner, and this can be an embarrassing and frustrating experience – hence (perhaps) the gradual escalation of tension in the conversation above.

Lastly, I think that all these points show us something about why philosophy can be (and, equally, can fail to be) an important thing to do. We've seen that the nature of philosophy, as we've described it in this chapter, means that philosophical questions can arise anywhere and everywhere, simply because we can always step back and ask questions about the framework from within which we're thinking. Like Louis CK's daughter, we can always keep asking 'Why?' On the one hand, we've seen that this can make philosophy into a difficult and frustrating activity. And, let's face it, it also means that the space of possible philosophical inquiry will include some questions that we simply don't feel are worth bothering with. Life is short! Some of the frustration we might feel at the child, or the philosopher, who questions *everything* is surely legitimate – we could spend our time pondering the best way to think about shoelaces, or carpets, or jumpers, but aren't there more worthwhile things to do? So we should admit that a question's being philosophical in the sense I've been outlining doesn't necessarily mean it's important. However, I think that these very same features of philosophy also help us understand how philosophical questions can often be *extremely* important.

At various times throughout history the way people have gone about their business in the world has presupposed particular ways of thinking about things that, once they have been brought out into the open and examined, look clearly and disastrously wrong. For example, in the past, huge populations of people have gone along with practices of genocide, slavery and sexism. It seems to us now that as soon as we try to articulate a way of thinking about things according to which these practices look acceptable, we see that this can't be done. It looks to us now as if anyone who wholeheartedly went along with these practices must simply never have stepped back and tried to articulate *why* it was acceptable to kill, or enslave, or discriminate against, a class of people on the basis of their race, social standing or sex. For, if they'd done so, they would have realized that the way of thinking that these practices presuppose surely wasn't the *best* one – indeed, we now find it hard to see how any rational, well-functioning person *could* think in the ways required to make these practices seem OK. Because there are so many examples of trends and practices like this through history, surely we should also wonder whether *we* might be thinking about, and acting in, the world in ways that will seem crazy to future generations. Perhaps the ways we think about the relationship between mind and body (see Chapter 3), or about the role of religion in understanding our place in the world might seem strange and confused to future generations. Or perhaps the way we respond (or fail to respond) to the suffering of people in distant countries and cultures, or the ways in which we farm animals for food, will look as indefensible to future generations as some of the beliefs of our ancestors do to us. The best way for us to avoid having beliefs and practices that don't stand up to scrutiny, and that might ultimately be harmful to us and to others, is for us to engage in that scrutiny ourselves and see what happens. Stepping back, trying to get a clear view of how we currently *are* thinking about things, and seeing if we can replace that with a *better* way, has often been an important step on the way to improving how we live in and think about the world. And this is one important reason why philosophy can be a worthwhile thing to do.

How do we do it?

So, now we know something about what philosophy is, some of the kinds of questions it can ask, and why it can be an important thing to do. But how do we do it? What are the tools and methods that philosophers use to try to arrive at the right ways of thinking about things?

Here, I want to come back to something I said at the beginning of the chapter – just as the best way to really see what philosophy is all about is to work through this book, engaging with the questions you find in it, the best way to see what philosophers do is to work through the examples of philosophical positions and arguments that you'll find in the following chapters. However, even before doing this, I'll bet you already have a good idea of how to do philosophy. This is because, as we saw above, philosophy is something that we can't escape in our lives. All of us, sometimes, spend time stepping back and trying to work out the best way to think about things – how should we decide who we would vote for in the next election? How should we decide what we should be doing with our lives? How should I think about (or what should I do about) this strange feeling that comes over me whenever I'm in this person's company? We all have at least *some* idea of how we would try to answer questions like these, even if we find them very difficult. We look around for evidence (what do I know about the parties that I'm choosing between? What do I know about what makes a worthwhile life? What sort of feeling is it that I have when I'm with this person?). We think about how, or whether, the evidence we've got gives us good reasons to think or act in a particular way (do I like the values or policies of one of the parties in the election more than the other? If I think that making other people happy is the most worthwhile thing to do with my life, how can I do that best? If I feel this way whenever I'm with this person, but never think about them otherwise, then can it really be love that I'm feeling?). And we do our best to assess and weigh up these reasons in order to come to a decision about how to think or to act.

This activity – of stepping back and trying to think clearly and well about things – is just what we do when we engage in philosophy. But in philosophy, we make a special effort to make our thinking about the evidence, the reasons for thinking and acting that the evidence suggests, the conclusion we draw from weighing up those reasons, and the transition between each of these stages and the next, as clear and uncontroversial as we can. We try to continuously ask questions like: 'is this evidence really as it appears?'; 'does it really give us a reason to think in *this* way, rather than *that* way?'; 'are the reasons I've come up with really enough to show that my conclusion about how to think or act *must* be true?' In continuously asking questions like this, we're trying to make sure we're thinking about the issue at hand in the most clear and compelling way we can. For philosophers, this is the same as the task of trying to think about things in the right, or best, way – the task that, in this chapter, I'm identifying with philosophy.

In philosophy, this process of providing evidence and chains of reasoning that aim to demonstrate the truth of some claim or position is referred to as giving an **argument**. So while it's true that philosophers spend their time *arguing* for some position or other, we're not referring here to the type of 'arguing' that must be heated, bad-tempered or confrontational. Rather, we mean that philosophers spend their time trying to come up with evidence and chains of reasoning that point us toward the right way of thinking about something. A good way of understanding philosophical reasoning, in fact, is on the model of a mutually respectful conversation (rather than a bad-tempered argument). We try to put forward our views as clearly as we can, and listen sympathetically to questions or opposing views from our conversation partners. In response, we might be moved to defend, clarify, or modify our own views.

When doing philosophy, the conversation partners whom we're trying to get to share our views needn't be real, or present. We might instead be trying to clarify or convince ourselves of a view in response to some doubts or questions that we ourselves have. Or we might be considering how a past philosopher, or some other figure, might react to the views we hold and our reasons for holding them. This process of shaping and articulating our views in response to real or imagined others, such that we not only understand our own views better, but can explain to others why they're the right ones, is central to philosophy. It's no accident that Plato, the ancient Greek philosopher who's often held to be the starting point for Western philosophy (the philosopher A. N. Whitehead has described European philosophy as a series of footnotes to Plato) wrote most of his philosophical works as dialogues.

Now that we've clarified that the process of philosophical argumentation should be constructive and sympathetic, rather than adversarial, let's look at our first example of a philosophical argument, to give us a more concrete example of how to go about the kind of thinking characteristic of philosophy. One topic that philosophy has puzzled over for a long time is the question of what it means for us to be free, or to have 'free will'. It seems that, at any given moment, I have a lot of freedom as to what I decide to do or not do. For example, it seems to me that right at this moment I could stop writing this chapter and go and have a nice lie down, go to the pub or have a cup of tea – but I choose not to do any of these things. However, we can give the following simple argument that calls into question whether I'm really as free as I think I am. Our argument has three **premises** – that is, three claims that it puts forward in order to support its conclusion:

Premise 1. The way the world was in the past controls exactly how it is in the present, and how it will be in the future.
Premise 2. We are part of the world, just like everything else around us.
Premise 3. We can't control how things were in the past, or the way the past controls the present and the future.
Conclusion. Therefore, we don't control anything that happens in the world – including all the things that we think, say and do.

This is a surprising conclusion! Should we accept it? At first glance (and perhaps at several more), this argument looks convincing – it seems that if the premises are true then the conclusion must be true, or to put it another way, that the truth of the conclusion follows from the truth of the premises. When this is the case, we say that an argument, or form of reasoning is **valid**. Moreover, the premises above look pretty good! If we think that those premises are true, and that the argument is valid, then the conclusion must also be true. When this is true of an argument – when it is valid, with true premises (and therefore also has a true conclusion) – we say that the argument is **sound**.

So, do we have a sound argument here? Let's think of the ways we might question it. We could try to question the truth of one or more of the premises – for example, perhaps the past state of the world *doesn't* control exactly how it is in the present. Perhaps we can appeal to the sorts of considerations from quantum mechanics mentioned above (p. 4), to show that the world being some particular way in the past is compatible with many different ways that it could turn out to be in the future. Or we could question our second premise: perhaps we *aren't* parts of the world just like everything else. Perhaps there is something special about us and our minds, such that the laws that govern the rest of the world don't apply to everything that we think and do. We might even try to question the third premise: perhaps we *can* in some way control how things were in the past, or the laws that govern how the present and future states of the world unfold from past ones (this seems to me like the toughest option!).

Alternatively, instead of questioning the truth of the premises, we can question the validity of the argument, and deny that the truth of the premises guarantees the truth of the conclusion. Perhaps we could try to show that what we mean by 'control' when we say that the past state of the physical world 'controls' its future states is different from what we mean when we say that we are 'in control' of our actions. If there are really two different meanings, or senses, of control in play here, then perhaps what the premises of the argument tell us about the way the past controls the present doesn't really show us anything about whether or not we have 'control' over our actions. Of course, another option is to simply accept the conclusion, and then (presumably) to consider whether or how we should, in light of this, revise our understanding of ourselves and our relation to the world.

Now, I don't want to try to decide between these different possible reactions to this argument here – instead, you might like to try to think about which of the above lines of response, if any, seems the most compelling to you. For now, we can note that each of the above suggested responses to the argument has some work associated with it. For example, if we want to respond by denying the first premise through appealing to what we know about quantum mechanics, then we might still face problems explaining the sense in which we're free – if the way the past controls the future were random and unpredictable, then wouldn't this pose just as much of a problem for our control over our actions as is posed if the past controlled the future in a precise and determinate way? If we question the second premise, then we will need to say something about just how we are different from the rest of the things in the world – we will see some of the problems associated with this when we learn about **dualism** in Chapter 3. Or if we deny that the argument's conclusion follows from its premises, in the way I suggested earlier, then we will need to say something about the special sense of control I have over my own actions, and how it differs from the way the past states of the world control present and future states. This should remind us of some points we've seen already – making progress on philosophical problems is often hard, and our answers to philosophical questions will often suggest yet more questions that require answers.

In thinking about the example argument we've just considered, we were involved in working out the right way to think about the sense in which we're free, or in control of our actions. Thinking about our example (and thinking of philosophy on the model of a dialogue or conversation) brings out the fact that often our working out the right way to think about things will involve engaging with arguments and positions that other people have put forward – trying to identify and assess the premises that their views are based on, and the chains of reasoning that lead from those premises to their conclusions.

In working your way through this book, you'll meet many more arguments, and get a much richer idea of the different ways in which philosophical arguments can work, and can be questioned. But, for now, we should note that identifying and thinking through a philosophical question or argument isn't always as simple as the above example suggests. Above, we had a small number of easily digestible premises that were supposed to lead to the conclusion in a straightforward way. But we surely all recognize from our own experiences of working out the best way to think about difficult questions or topics, or trying to bring someone else into agreement with our way of thinking, that this isn't always how things go. Often we find ourselves fumbling around, not quite sure how to express ourselves, and puzzled about exactly how all the different considerations that seem relevant to us fit together.

Think, for example, about what I'm doing in writing this chapter. I'm putting forward a characterization of philosophy as the activity of working out the right way of thinking about things, and attempting to say what I mean by that, why I believe it, and why I think you should believe it too. So in doing this I am (and you are, if you're thinking these thoughts along with me) doing the philosophy of philosophy – I'm trying to articulate and explain the best way of thinking about philosophy. But note that, although my conclusion – the way I'm suggesting we should understand philosophy – might be easily stated, I haven't used clearly labelled and neatly expressed premises and chains of reasoning to get there. I've given some examples to illustrate what I mean; I've tried to respond to the possible objection that this definition blurs the boundaries between philosophy and other subjects; and I've tried to clarify (and support) what I mean by noting various features of philosophy that follow from it. Hopefully, the way I'm recommending we think about philosophy, and some of the reasons in favour of thinking of it in that way, are nevertheless coming across.

This goes to show that philosophical thinking and argument doesn't always have the neat and tidy structure we've just seen in the argument about free will. Often the premises and chains of reasoning involved are multiple, complex and overlapping – and often hard work is required to bring them out into the open so that we can assess them. But bringing them out into the open in this way is always what philosophy aims at, even in cases where our topic and our thinking about it is so complex and multifaceted that we can never make all the aspects of our thinking fully explicit. Even in these cases, our goal is still to get as clear a view as possible of our presuppositions, commitments and lines of reasoning, so that we can have the best chance of convincing ourselves and others that we are thinking about things in the right way.

Is there a 'right way' of thinking about things?

You might have some questions or reservations about the way I've defined philosophy so far. If so, good! This means that you're getting into the spirit of *doing* philosophy – of trying to work out for yourself what the right way of thinking about some topic or question is, by critically examining the assumptions and reasoning of yourself and others. One question that might occur to you about what I've been saying is what might be meant by the 'right way' to think about things. Isn't this disturbingly vague? How do we know that there *is* a right way, in any given case? And even if there is, how do we know it's the sort of thing we can arrive at by thinking about it? These are very important questions for philosophy – in doing philosophy, we try to find things out about ourselves and our place in the world by thinking things through in the ways I've started to describe. These questions ask whether there are really facts of the matter about the things we're thinking about that would determine what would count as the 'right way' of thinking about them; and they ask why we should be confident that the 'right way' of thinking is something we could arrive at by doing philosophy. As with our discussion of the argument about free will, I don't want to try to answer these questions here. But I do want to bring this chapter to its conclusion by quickly considering what two major figures in the history of philosophy have thought about them.

According to **David Hume** (1711–76), Edinburgh's most famous philosophical export, such a sceptical attitude to our capacity to find the truth about the world through philosophy would be entirely appropriate (we'll meet Hume again, and think about some of his ideas in more detail, in Chapter 5). For Hume, the most important constraint on philosophy is that it should stay completely faithful to what our experience of the world tells us. However, Hume thought that when we consider things carefully, our experience of the world doesn't tell us nearly as much as we think. For example, when we look at the world we *think* that we experience one event causing another – as when I see one billiard ball knock into another, and appear to cause it to roll away. But Hume argued that all we really experience is a series of impressions of billiard balls at various places and at various times, and that we never experience any additional 'causation' that links the events in this chain of impressions together. The idea of causation is something extra, that our minds add to the impressions we get from the world – and we have no good reason to believe that this causal way of thinking that we automatically fall into corresponds to the way the world really is. For Hume, this wasn't only the case for causation – he thought that almost *any* attempt to find truths about how the world is just by thinking about it is doomed. For Hume, 'the observation of human blindness and weakness is the result of all philosophy, and meets us at every turn, in spite of our endeavours to elude or avoid it' (Hume 1748/1975, 31). Our thinking can only ever reveal the particular habits that we happen to have of associating ideas and drawing conclusions, based on our impressions of the world. Whether these habits of thinking correspond well to the way the world actually is (and thus whether we have good reasons to believe that they're the *right* ways of thinking about things) is simply something we can never know.

The German philosopher **Immanuel Kant** (1724–1804) famously said that Hume's philosophy awoke him from his dogmatic slumbers. Previously, Kant had been content to simply *assume* that philosophical thinking can put us in touch with the way the world is (and thus allow us to arrive at the right way of thinking about things) – but after reading Hume, he realized that trying to *prove* that philosophical thinking was up to this job was crucial to showing that philosophy was a worthwhile pursuit. In Kant's monumental (and difficult!) book, *Critique of Pure Reason*, he set himself the task of showing that philosophy could reveal more than just the arbitrary rules and patterns that our thought happens to follow. His method of doing so is too complex and multi-faceted for me to try to summarize here, but his important claim is that the rules and patterns that our thought follows are also the rules and patterns that the world which we are thinking about follows. To give a very crude summary of his views, he thinks that this is the case because he thinks that the very idea of a world that *doesn't* conform to the rules and patterns of our mind is nonsensical. Philosophy does indeed, as Hume thought, identify ways in which we can't avoid thinking about and experiencing the world – e.g. as stretching through space, as unfolding over time, and as containing causally connected events. But these unavoidable facts about our thought are also facts about what it is for there to be a world present to think about in the first place. It doesn't really make sense for us to contemplate the possibility that the world might not match up to the ways we have of thinking about it (as involving space, time and causation), because as soon as we try to articulate this possibility, we're no longer contemplating something that we can call a world. To put the idea even more briefly, Kant argues that the world has to conform to the rules that our thought follows, because it turns out that those very same rules spell out what it takes for there to be a world present for us to think about.

Because of their different ideas about the power of human reason to put us in touch with the world, Hume and Kant had different ideas about the scope of philosophy. For Hume, as we just saw, the project of trying to work our way towards the 'best' way of thinking about things is futile. Although we might be able to come to a clear view of the way in which we do in fact think about things, Hume thought we simply couldn't address the question of whether that way of thinking was doing a good or a bad job of representing the world. Kant, on the other hand, thought that many of the important patterns in our ways of thinking about the world are just the right ones to put us in touch with the world, for the reasons I quickly sket-ched above. Because of this, the right way of thinking about things, for Kant, is the way that rational thinking would ultimately lead us to if we followed it to its proper conclusions. Now, these are complex ideas and arguments, and I haven't tried to do them full justice here. But I wanted to mention them because they illustrate how even the definition of philosophy that I've been offering in this chapter suggests further philosophical questions, about the scope of philosophy and the nature of the relationship between our mind and the world. And, just like the other philosophical questions we've considered so far, and which you'll go on to consider in the rest of this book, we try to address those questions by attempting to get a clear view of the evidence we have at our disposal, the reasons it gives us to think or believe certain things, and the conclusions that follow from those reasons. I said in the previous section that we can think of philosophy as like a dialogue, where we sympathetically listen to other points of view and test them against our own. And I noted there that our partners in the dialogue need not be ones who are actually present with us. In this section we've seen another of the exciting and challenging aspects of philosophy – in working out the right way to think about things we can quickly find ourselves in a kind of dialogue with great thinkers of the past such as Hume and Kant.

Conclusion

In the rest of this book, you'll get the chance to think in greater detail about some of the issues we've only touched on in this chapter. You'll consider the right ways to think about our knowledge, mind, morality, testimony, scientific theories and time travel. By thinking carefully and critically about these topics and the arguments you'll meet for them, you won't just be learning about philosophy – you'll be doing it. In this chapter, I've tried to say something about what I think that process involves. We've seen that philosophical questions can crop up anywhere, and that sometimes thinking clearly about them can be very important – as when it seems that we are thinking or acting in indefensible ways simply because we've failed to step back and attempt to get a clear view of what we're doing. The twentieth-century English philosopher Isaiah Berlin expresses these points well when he writes of philosophy:

> If it is objected that all this seems very abstract and remote from daily experience, something too little concerned with the central interests, the happiness and unhappiness and ultimate fate of ordinary [people], the answer is that this charge is false. [People] cannot live without seeking to describe and explain the universe to themselves. The models they use in doing this must deeply affect their lives, not least when they are unconscious; much of the misery and frustration of men is due to the mechanical or unconscious, as well as deliberate, application of models where they do not work.
>
> (1980: 10)

Philosophy aims to bring these models into the light, and to carefully and thoughtfully assess whether they are the ones we should actually be using. This, I think, is the sense in which philosophy truly is for everyone – philosophical questions arise and are important for us all, whether we choose to spend time addressing them or not. That's why I think that in working your way through this book, you will be investing time in an activity that is valuable for us all.

Chapter summary

- Philosophy is an activity, and to understand what it is, the best thing to do is to engage with the kinds of philosophical problems, questions and arguments found in this book.
- We can characterize philosophy as the activity of working out the right way to think about things.
- Philosophy is closely related to many academic disciplines, since they aim at thinking about things in the right way. But we can distinguish between doing those subjects and doing philosophy, by distinguishing between the thinking that goes on in those subjects and the activity of stepping back to assess whether the methods and presuppositions of that thinking are the right ones.
- These points about philosophy mean that philosophical questions can arise almost anywhere, can often concern giving reasons or justifications for ways of thinking and acting that we take for granted, and can often be difficult to answer.
- These points also suggest why philosophy can be an important thing to do – we can think of many cases where it seems that history might have been changed for the better if people had stepped back and attempted to justify their ways of thinking and acting to themselves.
- In doing philosophy we are usually concerned with giving or assessing arguments – that is, evidence and sequences of reasoning that lead to a conclusion. We try to give arguments that are both valid (meaning that if the premises of the argument are true then the conclusion must be true) and sound (meaning that they are valid, and that they have true premises – and therefore that their conclusion is true). We can criticize arguments by trying to show either that one or more of their premises is false (the argument is not sound), or that the truth of the conclusion does not follow from the premises (the argument is not valid).
- The question of what it means to think of things in the 'right way' is a difficult one. Hume had a sceptical view of the prospects of

philosophy, since he argued that philosophy can only show how we happen to think, not whether this corresponds to the way the world is. In response to Hume, Kant argued that we can uncover truths about the world through thinking alone, since the rules that govern our thinking are also the rules that govern the world.

Study questions

1 In this chapter I suggested that philosophy is the activity of working out the right way of thinking about things. Do you think this is a good definition of philosophy? Does it leave anything out that you think counts as philosophy? Or does it include anything that shouldn't count as philosophy? (It might be interesting to compare your answers to this question before and after you have read the rest of the book.)

2 What questions would we ask if we were doing the philosophy of mathematics, rather than doing mathematics?

3 Stephen Hawking recently upset philosophers by saying that science had replaced philosophy as a way of answering all the important questions about ourselves and the world. Do you think there are questions that science cannot answer, but that philosophy could?

4 Other than the examples we've considered in this chapter, can you give an example of a philosophical question that seems important? Can you give an example of one that seems unimportant?

5 Come up with an argument that is valid, but not sound. Now come up with an argument that is both valid and sound.

6 Which of the responses to the argument against free will in this chapter do you think is the most convincing? Why?

7 Whose account of the prospects of philosophy do you think is more convincing – Hume's or Kant's? Can you think of how Hume might reply to Kant?

Introductory further reading

Berlin, I. (1980) 'The Purpose of Philosophy', in his *Concepts and Categories: Philosophical Essays*, Oxford: Oxford University Press. (Excellent essay about the nature and purpose of philosophy, from which the quote in the concluding section above is drawn.)

Blackburn, S. (1999) *Think*, New York: Oxford University Press. (A great introduction to philosophy, covering many of its main branches.)

Hume, D. (1748/1975) *An Enquiry Concerning Human Understanding*, in *Enquiries Concerning Human Understanding and Concerning the Principles of*

Morals, ed. L. A. Selby-Bigge, 3rd edn, Oxford: Oxford University Press. (If you'd like to learn more about Hume's views on the mind and our knowledge of the world, his *Enquiries* are accessible and fun to read.)

Nagel, T. (1989) *What Does It All Mean?* New York: Oxford University Press. (Similar to Blackburn's *Think*, this is a short and extremely readable introduction to some of the main branches of philosophy.)

Rosenberg, J. (1996) *The Practice of Philosophy: A Handbook for Beginners*, Upper Saddle River, NJ: Prentice Hall. (An accessible introduction to philosophical argument form and how to think and write critically about philosophical arguments.)

Advanced further reading

Kant, I. (1787/1998) *Critique of Pure Reason*, trans. P. Guyer and A. Wood, New York: Cambridge University Press. (Kant is harder to read than Hume. But if you'd like to understand more about his ideas about the nature and limits of philosophy then the Prefaces and Introductions to his *Critique of Pure Reason*, are easier going than the rest of the book, and are good places to start. For a more accessible version, see Jonathan Bennett's excellent translation (and clarification), available at http://bit.ly/11WK vgl

Murdoch, I. (1970) *The Sovereignty of Good*, Bristol: Routledge & Kegan Paul. (Although this doesn't deal directly with ideas from this chapter, Murdoch's book is one of my favourite examples of philosophical writing. I've included it here because I think it's an excellent example of philosophy that manages to be clear, precise and careful while presenting a case that it's impossible to reduce to a straightforward series of premises and a conclusion.)

Russell, B. (1998) *The Problems of Philosophy*, Oxford: Oxford University Press. (A slightly more advanced introduction to philosophical problems and reasoning than those in the above section, but still accessible. Presents the problems of philosophy that appeared most pressing when this was originally written in 1912, but it's still a classic!)

Strawson, P. F. (1962) 'Freedom and Resentment', *Proceedings of the British Academy* 48: 1–25. (An influential paper arguing that our understanding of ourselves as free and responsible for our actions should not be undermined by the fact that the past controls the present and future.)

Internet resources

Joll, N. (2010) 'Contemporary Metaphilosophy', in B. Dowden and J. Fieser (eds) *Internet Encyclopedia of Philosophy* [online encyclopedia], www.iep. utm.edu/con-meta/. (A wide-ranging but accessible introduction to different approaches in the philosophy of philosophy over the past hundred or so years.)

'What Is Philosophy?', *Philosophy Bites* [blog], 14 November 2010, http:// philosophybites.com/2010/11/what-is-philosophy.html. (25 interesting minutes of contemporary philosophers attempting to say what they think philosophy is.)

20   *Dave Ward*

Plato's *Apology*, at *The Internet Classics Archive*, ed. D. C. Stevenson [website], http://classics.mit.edu/Plato/apology.html&. (Online text of Plato's dialogue where Socrates gives a speech defending the life devoted to philosophical enquiry that has resulted in his being sentenced to death.)

The Partially Examined Life [podcast], www.partiallyexaminedlife.com. (An entertaining podcast by a group of one-time philosophy postgraduates, on a different topic, figure or book every three weeks or so. Many episodes are relevant to this chapter: Episodes 1 and 2 on Plato's *Apology* (and philosophy in general), Episode 17 on Hume, Episode 19 on Kant, and Episode 73 on 'Why Do Philosophy?' Warning: contains occasional strong language!)

2 What is knowledge? Do we have any?

Duncan Pritchard

Introduction

This chapter introduces you to an area of philosophy called the 'theory of knowledge', also known as **epistemology**. In particular, we will be exploring two philosophical questions that are fundamental to epistemology. The first question is: what is the nature of knowledge? What is it that determines whether or not someone knows something? As we will see, this question is harder to answer than you might think. The second question is: do we have any knowledge? This second question concerns the philosophical problem of **radical scepticism**, which is the problem of demonstrating that we do have the knowledge we typically credit to ourselves. In its most extreme form, radical scepticism maintains that knowledge is simply impossible. As I hope to convince you, explaining just what is mistaken about radical scepticism is quite a challenge. We will take these two questions in turn, since we need to have a reasonable grip on what knowledge is before we can understand what it is the sceptic is claiming we don't possess.

Propositional knowledge versus ability knowledge

Think of all the things that you know, or at least think you know, right now. You know, for example, that the Earth is round and that Paris is the capital of France. You know that you can speak (or at least read) English, and that two plus two is equal to four. You know, presumably, that all bachelors are unmarried men, that it is wrong to hurt people just for fun, that *The Godfather II* is a wonderful film, and that the moon is not made of cheese. And so on.

But what is it that all these cases of knowledge have in common? Think again of the examples just given, which include geographical, linguistic, mathematical, aesthetic, ethical and scientific knowledge.

Given these myriad types of knowledge, what, if anything, ties them all together?

In all the examples of knowledge just given, the type of knowledge in question is what is called **propositional knowledge**, in that it is knowledge of a **proposition**. A proposition is what is asserted by a sentence which says that something is the case – e.g. that the Earth is flat, that bachelors are unmarried men, that 2 + 2 = 4, and so on. Propositional knowledge will be the focus of this section of the book, but we should also recognize from the outset that it is not the only sort of knowledge that we possess.

There is, for example, **ability knowledge**, or 'know-how'. Ability knowledge is clearly different from propositional knowledge; I know how to swim, for example, but I do not thereby know a set of propositions about how to swim. Indeed, I'm not altogether sure that I could tell you how to swim, but I do know how to swim nonetheless (and I could prove it by manifesting this ability – by jumping into a swimming pool and doing the breaststroke, say).

Ability knowledge is certainly an important type of knowledge to have. We want lots of know-how, such as knowing how to ride a bicycle, to drive a car, or to operate a personal computer. Notice, however, that while only relatively sophisticated creatures like humans possess propositional knowledge, ability knowledge is far more common. An ant might plausibly be said to know how to navigate its terrain, but would we want to say that an ant has propositional knowledge; that there are facts which the ant knows? Could the ant know, for example, that the terrain it is presently crossing is someone's porch? Intuitively not, and this marks out the importance of propositional knowledge over other types of knowledge like ability knowledge, which is that such knowledge presupposes the sort of relatively sophisticated intellectual abilities possessed by (mature) humans.

Henceforth, when we talk about knowledge, we will have propositional knowledge in mind.

Knowledge, truth and belief

Two things that just about every epistemologist agrees on are that a prerequisite for possessing knowledge is that one has a belief in the relevant proposition, and that that belief must be true. So if you know that Paris is the capital of France, then you must believe that this is the case, and your belief must also be true.

Take the belief requirement first. It is sometimes the case that we explicitly *contrast* belief and knowledge, as when we say things like,

'I don't merely believe that he was innocent, I know it', which might on the face of it be thought to imply that knowledge does not require belief after all. If you think about these sorts of assertions in a little more detail, however, then it becomes clear that the contrast between belief and knowledge is being used here simply to emphasize the fact that one *not only* believes the proposition in question, but *also* knows it. In this way, these assertions actually lend support to the claim that knowledge requires belief, rather than undermining it.

In order to further assess the plausibility of the belief requirement for knowledge, imagine for a moment that it didn't hold. This would mean that one could have knowledge of a proposition that one did not even believe. Suppose, for example, that someone claimed to have known a quiz answer, even though it was clear from that person's behaviour at the time that she didn't even believe the proposition in question (perhaps she put forward a different answer to the question, or no answer at all). Clearly we would not agree that this person did have knowledge in this case. The reason for this relates to the fact that to say that someone has knowledge is to credit that person with a certain kind of success. But for it to be *your* success, then belief in the proposition in question is essential, since otherwise this success is not creditable to you at all.

Next, consider the truth requirement. In particular, is it plausible to suppose that one could know a false proposition? Of course, we often *think* that we know something and then it turns out that we were wrong, but that's just to say that we didn't really know it in the first place. Could we genuinely know a false proposition? Could I know, for example, that the moon is made of cheese, even though it manifestly isn't? I take it that when we talk of someone having knowledge, we mean to exclude such a possibility. This is because to ascribe knowledge to someone is to credit that person with having got things right, and that means that what we regard that person as knowing had better not be false, but true.

Note that in saying that knowledge requires true belief we should be careful to be clear that we are *not* thereby saying that knowledge requires infallibility, such that there is no possibility of one making a mistake in this regard. Presumably, you know what you had for breakfast this morning. The claim that knowledge requires true belief entails therefore that your belief about what you had for breakfast this morning is true. But a subject matter like what you had for breakfast this morning is certainly the kind of thing that one could be in error about. That knowledge requires true belief just means that you are not in fact in error in this case; it does not mean that you couldn't have possibly been in error (i.e. if things had been different, such as if someone had tricked you by switching your breakfast cereals around, say).

Knowledge versus mere true belief

It is often noted that belief *aims* at the truth, in the sense that when we believe a proposition, we believe it to be the case (i.e. to be true). When what we believe is true, then there is a match between what we think is the case and what is the case. We have got things right. If mere true belief suffices for 'getting things right', however, then one might wonder as to why epistemologists do not end their quest for an account of knowledge right there and simply hold that knowledge is nothing more than true belief (i.e. 'getting things right').

There is in fact a very good reason why epistemologists do not rest content with mere true belief as an account of knowledge, and that is that one can gain true belief entirely by *accident*, in which case it would be of no credit to you at all that you got things right. Consider Harry, who forms his belief that the horse Lucky Lass will win the next race purely on the basis of the fact that the name of the horse appeals to him. Clearly this is not a good basis on which to form one's belief about the winner of the next horse race, since whether or not a horse's name appeals to you has no bearing on its performance.

Suppose, however, that Harry's belief turns out to be true, in that Lucky Lass *does* win the next race. Is this knowledge? Intuitively not, since it is just a matter of *luck* that his belief was true in this case. Remember that knowledge involves a kind of success that is creditable to the agent. Crucially, however, successes that can be put down to mere luck are never credited to the agent.

To emphasize this point, think for a moment about successes in another realm, such as archery. Notice that if one genuinely is a skilled archer, then if one tries to hit the bullseye, and the conditions are right (e.g. the wind is not gusting), then one usually *will* hit the bullseye. That's just what it means to be a skilled archer. The word 'usually' is important here, since someone who isn't a skilled archer might, as it happens, hit the bullseye on a particular occasion, but she wouldn't *usually* hit the bullseye under these conditions. Perhaps, for example, she aims her arrow and, by luck, it hits the centre of the target. Does the mere fact that she is successful on this one occasion mean that she is a skilled archer? No, and the reason is that she would not be able to repeat this success. If she tried again, for example, her arrow would in all likelihood sail off into the heavens.

Having knowledge is just like this. Imagine that one's belief is an arrow, which is aimed at the centre of the target, truth. Hitting the bullseye and forming a true belief suffices for getting things right, since all this means is that one was successful on that occasion. It does not suffice, however, for having knowledge any more than hitting the bullseye purely by chance indicates that you are skilled in archery. To have knowledge, one's success must genuinely be the result of one's efforts, rather than merely being by chance. Only then is that success attributable to one. And this means that forming one's belief in the way that one does ought, usually, and in those circumstances, to lead to a true belief.

Harry, who forms his true belief that Lucky Lass will win the race simply because he likes the name, is like the person who happens to hit the bullseye, but who is not a skilled archer. Usually, forming one's belief about whether a horse will win a race simply by considering whether the name of the horse appeals to you will lead you to form a false belief.

Contrast Harry with someone who genuinely knows that Lucky Lass will win the race. Perhaps, for example, this person is a 'Mr Big', a gangster who has fixed the race by drugging the other animals so that his horse, Lucky Lass, will win. He knows that the race will be won by Lucky Lass because the way he has formed his belief, by basing it on the special grounds he has for thinking that Lucky Lass cannot lose, would normally lead him to have a true belief. It is not a matter of luck that Mr Big hits the target of truth.

The challenge for epistemologists is thus to explain what needs to be added to mere true belief in order to get knowledge. In particular, epistemologists need to explain what needs to be added to true belief to capture this idea that knowledge, unlike mere true belief, involves a success that may be credited to the agent, where this means, for example, that the agent's true belief was not simply a matter of luck.

The classical account of knowledge

So it seems that there must be more to knowledge than just true belief. But what could this additional component be? The natural answer to this question, one that is often ascribed to the ancient Greek philosopher Plato (*c.*427–*c.*347 BC), is that what is needed is a *justification* for one's belief, where this is understood as being in possession of good reasons for thinking that what one believes is true. This proposal is known as the **classical account of knowledge**. (It is also sometimes referred to as the 'tripartite' – i.e. three-part – account of knowledge.)

Consider again the case of Harry, who believes that Lucky Lass will win the race because he likes the name, and Mr Big, who forms the same belief on the grounds that he has fixed the race. As we noted, although both of these agents believe truly, intuitively only Mr Big has knowledge of what he believes. The claim that it is justification that marks the difference between knowledge and mere true belief accords with this assessment of our two agents' beliefs. Mr Big, after all, has excellent reasons in support of his true belief, since he is aware that the other horses have been drugged and so don't have a hope of winning (unlike the undrugged Lucky Lass). Harry, in contrast, can't offer any good reasons in support of his belief. That he happens to like the name of a horse is hardly a good reason for thinking that this horse will win a race!

Plausibly, then, the missing ingredient in our account of knowledge is justification, such that knowledge is justified true belief. Indeed, until relatively recently most epistemologists thought that this theory of knowledge was correct. Unfortunately, as we will now see, the classical account of knowledge cannot be right, even despite its surface plausibility.

The Gettier problem

The person who demonstrated that the classical account of knowledge is untenable was a philosopher named Edmund Gettier (b. 1927). In a very short article (just two-and-a-half pages in length) he offered a devastating set of counterexamples to the classical account – what are now known as **Gettier cases**. In essence, what Gettier showed was that you could have a justified true belief and yet still lack knowledge of what you believe because your true belief was ultimately gained via luck in much the same way as Harry's belief was gained by luck.

We will use a different example from the ones cited by Gettier, though one that has the same general structure. Imagine a man, let's call him John, who comes downstairs one morning and sees that the grandfather clock in the hall says '8.20'. On this basis John comes to believe that it is 8.20 a.m., and this belief is true, since it *is* 8.20 a.m. Moreover, John's belief is justified in that it is based on excellent grounds. For example, John usually comes downstairs in the morning about this time, so he knows that the time is about right. Moreover, this clock has been very reliable at telling the time for many years and John has no reason to think that it is faulty now. He thus has good reasons for thinking that the time on the clock is correct.

Suppose, however, that the clock had, unbeknownst to him, stopped 24 hours earlier, so that John is now forming his justified true belief by looking at a stopped clock. Intuitively, if this were so then John would lack knowledge even though he has met the conditions laid down by the classical account of knowledge. After all, that John has a true belief in this case is, ultimately, a matter of luck, just like Harry's belief that Lucky Lass would win the 4.20 at Kempton.

If John had come downstairs a moment earlier or a moment later – or if the clock had stopped at a slightly different time – then he would have formed a false belief about the time by looking at this clock. Thus we can conclude that knowledge is not simply justified true belief.

There is a general form to all Gettier cases, and once we know this we can use it to construct an unlimited number of them. To begin with, we need to note that you can have a justified false belief, since this is crucial to the Gettier cases. For example, suppose you formed a false belief by looking at a clock that you had no reason for thinking wasn't working properly but which was, in fact, and unbeknownst to you, not working properly. This belief would clearly be justified, even though it is false. With this point in mind, there are three stages to constructing your own Gettier case.

First, you take an agent who forms her belief in a way that would usually lead her to have a false belief. In the example above, we took the case of someone looking at a stopped clock in order to find out the time. Clearly, using a stopped clock to find out the time would usually result in a false belief.

Second, you add some detail to the example to ensure that the agent's belief is justified nonetheless. In the example above, the detail we added was that the agent had no reason for thinking that the clock wasn't working properly (the clock is normally reliable, is showing what appears to be the right time, and so on), thus ensuring that her belief is entirely justified.

Finally, you make the case such that while the way in which the agent formed her belief would normally have resulted in a justified false belief, in this case it so happened that the belief was true. In the stopped clock case, stipulating that the stopped clock just happens to be 'telling' the right time does this.

Putting all this together, we can construct an entirely new Gettier case from scratch. As an example of someone forming a belief in a way that would normally result in a false belief, let's take someone who forms her belief that Madonna is across the street by looking at a life-sized cardboard cut-out of Madonna which is advertising her forthcoming tour, and which is posted just across the street. Forming one's belief about whether someone is across the street by looking at a life-sized cut-out of that person would not normally result in a true belief. Next, we add some detail to the example to ensure that the belief is justified. In this case we can just stipulate that the cut-out is very authentic looking, and that there is nothing about it which would obviously give away the fact that it is a cardboard cut-out – it does not depict Madonna in an outrageous costume that she wouldn't plausibly wear on a normal street, for example. The agent's belief is thus justified. Finally, we make the scenario such that the belief is true. In this case, for instance, all we need to do is stipulate that, as it happens, Madonna *is* across the street, doing some window-shopping out of view of our agent. *Voilà*, we have constructed our very own Gettier case!

Responding to the Gettier problem

There is no easy way to respond to the Gettier cases, and since Gettier's article back in 1963, a plethora of different theories of knowledge have been developed in order to offer an account of knowledge that is Gettier-proof. Initially, it was thought that all one needed to do to deal with these cases is simply to tweak the classical account of knowledge. For instance, one proposal was that in order to have knowledge, one's true belief must be justified and also not in any way based on false presuppositions, such as, in the case of John just described, the false presupposition that the clock is working and not stopped. There is a pretty devastating problem with this sort of proposal, however, which is that it is difficult to spell out this idea of a 'presupposition' such that it is strong enough to deal with Gettier cases and yet not so strong that it prevents us from having most of the knowledge that we think we have.

For example, suppose that John has a sister across town – let's call her Sally – who is in fact at this moment finding out what the time is by looking at a working clock. Intuitively, Sally *does* gain knowledge of what the time is by looking at the time on the clock. Notice, however, that Sally may believe all sorts of other related propositions, some of which may be false – for example, she may believe that the clock is regularly maintained, when in fact no one is taking care of it. Is this belief a presupposition of her belief in what the time is? If it is (i.e. if we understand the notion of a 'presupposition' liberally) then this false presupposition will prevent her from having knowledge of the time, even though we would normally think that looking at a reliable working clock is a great way of coming to know what the time is.

Alternatively, suppose we understand the notion of a 'presupposition' in a more restrictive way such that this belief isn't a presupposition of Sally's belief in the time. The problem now is to explain why John's false belief that he's looking at a working clock counts as a pre-supposition of his belief in the time (and so prevents him from counting as knowing what the time is) if Sally's false belief that the clock is regularly maintained is not also treated as a presupposition. Why don't they *both* lack knowledge of what the time is?

If this problem weren't bad enough, there is also a second objection to this line of response to the Gettier cases, which is that it is not clear that the agent in a Gettier case need presuppose *anything* at all. Consider a different Gettier case in this regard, due to Chisholm. In this example, we have a farmer – let's call her Gayle – who forms her belief that there is a sheep in the field by looking at a shaggy dog, which happens to look just like a sheep. As it turns out, however, there is a sheep in the field (standing behind the dog), and hence Gayle's belief is true. Moreover, her belief is also justified because she has great evidence for thinking that there is a sheep in the field (she can see what looks to be a sheep in the field, for example).

Given the immediacy of Gayle's belief in this case, however, it is hard to see that it really presupposes any further beliefs at all, at least unless we are to understand the notion of a presupposition *very* liberally. And notice that if we do understand the notion of a presupposition so liberally that Gayle counts as illicitly making a presupposition, the problem then re-emerges of how to account for apparently genuine cases of knowledge, such as, intuitively, that possessed by Sally.

The dilemma for proponents of this sort of response to the Gettier cases is thus to explain how we should understand the notion of a presupposition broadly enough so that it applies to the Gettier cases while at the same time understanding it narrowly enough so that it doesn't apply to other non-Gettier cases in which, intuitively, we would regard the agent concerned as having knowledge. In short, we want a response to the problem, which explains why John lacks knowledge in such a way that it doesn't thereby deprive Sally of knowledge.

Once it was recognized that there was no easy answer to the problem posed to the classical account of knowledge by the Gettier cases, the race was on to find a radically new way of analysing knowledge which was Gettier-proof. One feature that all such accounts share is that they understand the conditions for knowledge such that they demand more in the way of cooperation from the world than simply that the belief in question is true. That is, on the classical account of knowledge there is one condition which relates to the world – the truth condition – and two conditions that relate to us as agents – the belief and justification conditions. These last two conditions, at least as they are usually understood in any case, don't demand anything from the world, in the sense that they could obtain regardless of how the world is. If I were the victim of an hallucination, for example, then I might have a whole range of wholly deceptive experiences, experiences that, nonetheless, lead me to believe something and, moreover, to justifiably believe it. (For example, if I seem to see that, say, there is a glass in front of me, then this is surely a good, and thus justifying, reason for believing that there is a glass in front of me, even if the appearance of the glass is an illusion.) The moral of the Gettier cases is, however, that you need to demand more from the world than simply that one's justified belief is true if you are to have knowledge.

In the stopped-clock Gettier case, for example, the problem came about because, although John had excellent grounds for believing what he did, it nevertheless remained that he did not know what he believed because of some oddity in the world – in this case that the normally reliable clock had not only stopped but had stopped in such a way that John still formed a true belief. It thus appears that we need an account of knowledge which imposes a further requirement on the world over and above the truth of the target belief – that, for example, the agent is, *in fact*, forming his belief in the right kind of way. But specifying exactly what this requirement involves is far from easy.

Radical scepticism

As it is usually understood in the contemporary debate, radical scepticism is not supposed to be thought of as a philosophical position (i.e. as a stance that someone adopts) as such, but rather it is meant as a challenge which any theorist of knowledge must overcome. That is, radical scepticism is meant to serve a *methodological* function. The goal is to show that one's theory of knowledge is scepticism-proof, since if it isn't – if it allows that most knowledge is impossible – then there must be something seriously wrong with the view. Accordingly we are not to think of the 'sceptic' as a person – as someone who is trying to convince us of anything – but rather as our intellectual conscience which is posing a specific kind of problem for our epistemological position in order to tease out what our view really involves and whether it is a plausible stance to take.

There are two main components to sceptical arguments, as they are usually understood in the contemporary discussion of this topic. The first component concerns what is known as a **sceptical hypothesis**. A sceptical hypothesis is a scenario in which you are radically deceived about the world and yet your experience of the world is exactly as it would be if you were not radically deceived. Consider, for example, the fate of the protagonist in the film *The Matrix*, who comes to realize that his previous experiences of the world were in fact being 'fed' into his brain although his body was confined to a large vat. Accordingly, albeit he seemed to be experiencing a world rich with interaction between himself and other people, in fact he was not interacting with anybody or any *thing* at all (at least over and above the tubes in the vat that were 'feeding' him his experiences), but was instead simply floating motionlessly. Call this the *brain-in-a-vat* sceptical hypothesis.

The problem posed by sceptical hypotheses is that we seem unable to know that they are false. After all, if our experience of the world could be exactly as it is and yet we are the victims of a sceptical hypothesis, then on what basis could we ever hope to distinguish a genuine experience of the world from an illusory one? How could one know that one is not a brain in a vat, given that one can't possibly tell the difference between the experiences one would have in the vat and the experiences one would have if everything were perfectly normal? The first key claim of the sceptical argument is thus that we are unable to know that we are not the victims of sceptical hypotheses.

The second component of the sceptical argument involves the claim that if we are unable to know the denials of sceptical hypotheses, it follows that we are unable to know very much at all. Right now, for example, I think that I know that I am sitting here at my desk writing this chapter. Given that I do not know that I am not the victim of a sceptical hypothesis, however, and given that if I were the victim of a sceptical hypothesis the world would appear exactly the same as it is just now even though I am *not* presently sitting at my desk, then how can I possibly know that I am sitting at my desk? The problem is that, so long as I cannot rule out sceptical hypotheses, I don't seem able to know very much at all.

We can roughly express this sceptical argument in the following way:

Premise 1. We are unable to know the denials of sceptical hypotheses.
Premise 2. If we are unable to know the denials of sceptical hypotheses, then we are unable to know anything of substance about the world.
Conclusion. Hence, we are unable to know anything of substance about the world.

Two very plausible claims about our knowledge can thus be used to generate a cogent argument which produces this rather devastating radically sceptical conclusion. In this sense, the sceptical argument is a paradox – i.e. a series of apparently intuitive premises, which together entail an absurd, and thus *counter-intuitive*, conclusion.

We've already noted the strong support that the first premise has, in that it does seem that one couldn't possibly know that one was not the victim of a sceptical hypothesis, such as the brain in a vat hypothesis. One might thus think that the weakest link in this argument must be the second premise.

Here is one basis on which one might dispute the second premise. Doesn't it look too demanding? That is, doesn't it ask far too much of a knower that she be able to rule out radical sceptical hypotheses if she is to have widespread knowledge of the world around her? Why should it be, for example, that in order for me to be properly said to know that I am sitting at my desk right now, I must first be able to rule out the possibility that I am a brain in a vat being 'fed' my experiences by futuristic supercomputers that are out to deceive me? Surely all that I need to do in order to have knowledge in this case is to form my belief in the right kind of way and for that belief to be supported by the appropriate evidence (e.g. that I can see my desk before me). To demand more than this seems perverse, and if scepticism merely reflects unduly restrictive epistemic standards then it isn't nearly as problematic as it might at first seem. We can reject *perverse* epistemic standards with impunity – it is only the *intuitively correct ones* that we need to pay serious attention to.

But this is too quick, for notice that it can't be true both that I am sitting here at my desk and that I am a brain in a vat (since brains in a vat do not 'sit' anywhere). Thus, if I know that I am sitting down at my desk then it seems I must also be able to know that I'm not a brain in a vat. After all, I know that if I am sitting down at my desk then I can't be a brain in a vat, and supposedly I do know that I am sitting down at my desk. So surely I must be able to know that I am not a brain in a vat too, right? (Consider the following parallel argument. One can either be sitting down or standing up, one can't do both. So if one knows that one is sitting down, then surely one can thereby know that one is not standing up, since one knows that one's sitting down excludes the possibility that one is standing up.)

Of course the problem with all of this is that we've already granted to the sceptic, in the first premise, that we can't know the denials of sceptical hypotheses, such as that one is a brain in a vat. It follows that if having knowledge of something so mundane as that one is seated at one's desk entails that one knows that one is not a brain in a vat, then one can't possibly have this mundane knowledge after all. So we are back with our original problem of explaining which of two premises that make up this argument is false.

The problem of radical scepticism therefore seems to turn on very plausible claims which are hard to deny, and this means that responding to this problem is easier said than done. So, not only is it difficult to explain what knowledge is (on account of the Gettier problem), but it is also difficult to demonstrate that we have much of the knowledge that we take ourselves to have (on account of the problem of radical scepticism). In this chapter we have thus witnessed, at least in broad outline, two of the most important problems of contemporary epistemology.

Chapter summary

- Epistemology is the theory of knowledge. One of the characteristic questions of epistemology concerns what all the myriad kinds of knowledge we ascribe to ourselves have in common: *What is knowledge?*

- We can distinguish between knowledge of propositions, or *propositional knowledge*, and know-how, or *ability knowledge*. Intuitively, the former demands a greater degree of intellectual sophistication on the part of the knower than the latter.

- In order to have knowledge of a proposition, that proposition must be true, and one must believe it.

- Mere true belief does not suffice for knowledge, however, since one can gain mere true belief purely by luck, and yet you cannot gain knowledge purely by luck.

- According to the *classical account of knowledge*, knowledge is understood as justified true belief, where a justification for one's belief consists of good reasons for thinking that the belief in question is true.

- *Gettier cases* are cases in which one forms a true justified belief and yet lacks knowledge because the truth of the belief is largely a matter of luck. (The example we gave of this was that of someone forming a true belief about what the time is by looking at a stopped clock, which just so happens to be displaying the right time.) Gettier cases show that the classical account of knowledge in terms of justified true belief is unsustainable.

- There is no easy answer to the Gettier cases; no simple way of supplementing the classical account of knowledge so that it can deal with these cases. Instead, a radically new way of understanding knowledge is required, one that demands greater cooperation on the part of the world than simply that the belief in question be true.

- *Radical scepticism* is the view that it is impossible to know very much. We are not interested in the view because anyone positively defends it as a serious position, but rather because examining the sorts of considerations that can be put forward in favour of radical scepticism helps us to think about what knowledge is.

- One dominant type of sceptical argument appeals to what is known as a *sceptical hypothesis*. This is a scenario, which is indistinguishable from normal life but in which one is radically deceived (e.g. the possibility that one is a disembodied brain floating in a vat of nutrients, being 'fed' one's experiences by supercomputers).
- Using sceptical hypotheses, the sceptic can reason in the following way. I'm unable to know that I'm not the victim of a sceptical hypothesis (since such a scenario is indistinguishable from normal life), and thus it follows that I can't know any of the propositions that I think I know which are inconsistent with sceptical hypotheses (e.g. that I'm presently sitting writing this chapter).

Study questions

1 Explain, in your own words, what the difference is between ability knowledge and propositional knowledge, and give two examples of each.
2 What does it mean to say that knowledge requires true belief, and why do epistemologists claim that this the case?
3 Why is mere true belief not sufficient for knowledge? Give an example of your own of a case in which an agent truly believes something, but does not know it.
4 What is the classical account of knowledge? How does the classical account of knowledge explain why a lucky true belief doesn't count as knowledge?
5 What is a Gettier case, and what do such cases show? Try to formulate a Gettier case of your own.
6 In what way might it be said that the problem with Gettier cases is that they involve a justified true belief which is based on a false presupposition? Explain, with an example, why one cannot straightforwardly deal with the Gettier cases by advancing a theory of knowledge which demands justified true belief that does not rest on any false presuppositions.
7 What is a sceptical hypothesis, and what role does it play in sceptical arguments? Try to formulate a sceptical hypothesis of your own and use it as part of a radical sceptical argument.

Introductory further reading

Greco, J. (2007) 'External World Skepticism', *Philosophy Compass* 2, no 4: 624–95. (A sophisticated, yet still accessible, survey of the main issues as regards scepticism of the variety that concerns us in this chapter.)

Luper, S. (2010) 'Cartesian Skepticism', S. Bernecker and D. H. Pritchard (eds) *The Routledge Companion to Epistemology*, London: Routledge. (An authoritative and completely up-to-date survey of the kind of scepticism that is of interest to us in this chapter.)

Pritchard, D. (2013) *What Is This Thing Called Knowledge?*, 3rd edn, London: Routledge. (See Parts I and IV for a fuller, but still accessible, discussion of the nature of knowledge and the problem of radical scepticism.)

Steup, M., Turri, J. and Sosa, E. (eds) (2013) *Contemporary Debates in Epistemology*, 2nd edn, Oxford: Blackwell. (This volume contains a number of sections that would be relevant to the topics covered in this chapter. See especially the exchange between Jonathan Vogel and Richard Fumerton on scepticism (§5), and the exchange between Duncan Pritchard and Stephen Hetherington on whether there can be lucky knowledge (§7).)

Advanced further reading

Gettier, E. (1963) 'Is Justified True Belief Knowledge?', *Analysis* 23: 121–23, www.ditext.com/gettier/gettier.html. (The article which started the contemporary debate about how best to define knowledge and which contains, by definition, the first official Gettier cases.)

Hetherington, S. (2010) 'The Gettier Problem', chapter 12 of S. Bernecker and D. H. Pritchard (eds) *The Routledge Companion to Epistemology*, London: Routledge. (A very useful and up-to-date survey of the main issues raised by Gettier-style examples.)

Pritchard, D. (2009) *Knowledge*, Basingstoke: Palgrave Macmillan. (This is an advanced textbook in epistemology. Chapters 1–4 offer a critical overview of some of the main analyses of knowledge in the contemporary literature; chapter 6 presents the main themes in the contemporary debate regarding radical scepticism.)

Shope, R. K. (2002) 'Conditions and Analyses of Knowing', in P. K. Moser (ed.) *The Oxford Handbook of Epistemology*, Oxford: Oxford University Press, pp. 25–70. (A comprehensive treatment of the problem posed by Gettier cases and the various contemporary responses to that problem in the literature. The discussion that starts on p. 29 is most relevant to this chapter. Note that as Shope's book develops, it becomes increasingly more demanding.)

Zagzebski, L. (1999) 'What Is Knowledge?', in J. Greco and E. Sosa (eds) *The Blackwell Companion to Epistemology*, Oxford: Blackwell, pp. 92–116. (A very thorough overview of the issues surrounding the project of defining knowledge, especially in the light of the Gettier cases.)

Internet resources

Hetherington, S. (2005) 'Gettier Problems', in B. Dowden and J. Fieser (eds) *Internet Encyclopedia of Philosophy* [online encyclopedia], www.iep.utm.edu/

g/gettier.htm. (An excellent overview of the Gettier problem, and the main responses to it, by one of the leading epistemologists.)

Ichikawa, J. and Steup, M. (2012) 'The Analysis of Knowledge', in E. Zalta (ed.) *Stanford Encyclopedia of Philosophy* [online encyclopedia], http://plato. stanford.edu/entries/knowledge-analysis/. (An excellent and comprehensive overview of the issues regarding the project of defining knowledge.)

Klein, P. (2010) 'Skepticism', in E. Zalta (ed.) *Stanford Encyclopedia of Philosophy* [online encyclopedia], http://plato.stanford.edu/entries/skepticism/. (A superb overview of the literature on scepticism, written by one of the world's foremost epistemologists.)

Pritchard, D. (2002) 'Contemporary Skepticism', in B. Dowden and J. Fieser (eds) *Internet Encyclopedia of Philosophy* [online encyclopedia], www.iep. utm.edu/s/skepcont.htm. (An accessible introduction to the literature on scepticism.)

Truncellito, D. (2007) 'Epistemology', in B. Dowden and J. Fieser (eds) *Internet Encyclopedia of Philosophy* [online encyclopedia], www.iep.utm.edu/e/epistemo.htm. (Read up to the end of §2.b for more on the basic requirements for knowledge.)

3   What is it to have a mind?

Jane Suilin Lavelle

Introduction

What is it to have a mind? I'm certain that anyone reading this book
has a mind, and I am certain that tennis balls do not have minds. But
what are the special properties we consider 'minded' beings to have?
Do other animals or human infants share them? Is it possible for non-
organic things like computers to have these properties? This chapter
considers some answers to the question of what it is to have a mind
(henceforth *the Question*).

We begin by examining the claim that minds are made of a substance
which is completely different from the stuff that our bodies are made of.
This view has become known as **Cartesian dualism** (or 'substance
dualism') after its most famous proponent, the French philosopher
René Descartes (1596–1650). It is dualistic because it posits two kinds
of substance: **material substances** occupy a certain amount of space
(and our bodies and everything else in the world are composed of
them), while **immaterial substances** do not occupy any space. According to Cartesian dualism, minds are made of immaterial 'thinking'
substance which does not occupy space. As a consequence, the part of
me that thinks exists independently of the body. Cartesian dualism
answers *the Question* by claiming that having a mind requires having
an immaterial 'thinking' substance.

Few contemporary philosophers defend Cartesian dualism. However,
it is important to understand the shortcomings of this view in order to
properly grasp the significance of the theories of mind which followed
it. This is a technique frequently employed by philosophers facing a
tricky question: by understanding why a particular answer to a question
fails, one is then in a better position to try to construct a new answer
that does not fail in the same way. As we will see, certain philosophers
thought that Descartes' dualistic approach to *the Question* was the root

of its failure to provide an adequate answer and that a better strategy would be to claim that there is only one type of substance of which everything, including minds, is constituted. We will examine two different ways of developing this strategy.

Through exploring the transition from Cartesian dualism to views which only posit one kind of substance we will gain the conceptual tools we need to tackle a different kind of answer to *the Question*. It is common practice in philosophy, psychology and related disciplines to treat the mind as a kind of computer. We explore their reasons for doing so in the second half of this chapter.

A word of warning before we continue: much has been written about the issues discussed in this chapter and my aim is simply to give you some insight into a few of the formative questions in this field. At times I will relegate to a passing remark questions that philosophers have devoted their entire lives to examining. This is not to demean the importance of these issues, and where I can I will point you to other resources which explore them more carefully and rigorously than I am able to do here.

What we want from an account of the mind

'Hallo!' said Piglet, 'what are *you* doing?'
'Hunting', said Pooh.
'Hunting what?'
'Tracking something', said Winnie-the-Pooh very mysteriously.
'Tracking what?' said Piglet, coming closer.
'That's just what I ask myself. I ask myself, What?'
'What do you think you'll answer?'
'I shall have to wait until I catch up with it', said Winnie-the-Pooh.
(A. A. Milne, *Winnie-the-Pooh*)

Before we begin our hunt for an account of the mind it is helpful to think about some features that we believe minds to have, in case we pass over a perfectly good description of mindedness without recognizing it as such. Here are two features which an account of the mind should explain.

1 Causation

I want to drink tea and believe that there is tea in my mug, and this causes me to reach across my desk to pick up my mug. I believe that there is a student outside my office waiting to see me, so I open the door to greet her. I have a headache, so I take some aspirin.

These, hopefully mundane, examples are intended to demonstrate how central causation is to our concept of the mind. We should be suspicious if someone published an account of what it is to have a mind which could not explain how it is that my thoughts can cause me to act, and how I can alter my thoughts by altering the state of my body (taking hallucinogens changes the chemical state of my brain and also changes my thoughts). So our first requirement for an account of the mind is that it explain how my **mental states** can bring about changes in my body (my desire for tea, in combination with various other mental states, brings about my reaching for my mug), and how changing physical states of my body can effect changes in my mental states (e.g. taking an aspirin relieves my headache). I will use the term 'mental state' or 'psychological state' to refer to any mental phenomenon, e.g. thoughts, emotions, sensations. The hunger I feel when I want bacon, and the joy I feel in biting into a bacon sandwich, are examples of mental states.

2 *'Aboutness'*

It is clear that my thoughts are about things. Sometimes they are about actual states of affairs: I can think about how hungry I am or about the wallpaper in the hallway. Thoughts can also be about merely possible states of affairs: I can think about whether I want to go to the hills or the beach this weekend. Thoughts can even be about things which are impossible: I can think about what a five-legged fire-breathing unicorn might do if released in the city centre or whether I could tame such a creature and ride it. So the second feature an account of the mind should accommodate is how it is that we can have thoughts about things.

These criteria are the least controversial. However, there is a third feature which we intuitively associate with mindedness: in our search for what it is to be minded, surely we should be looking for something that is *conscious*. An account of the mind which does not touch on consciousness is simply ignoring the most obvious feature which demands explanation.

There are reasons for leaving consciousness off this list which you may accept or reject as you will. The first is that consciousness is notoriously difficult to characterize. Perhaps the most well-known articulation comes from Thomas Nagel's 1974 paper 'What Is it Like to Be a Bat?' Consciousness is the 'what-it's-likeness' to have certain psychological states. There is something it is like to listen to a symphony orchestra, to smell baking bread, or to see a red rose, however, pinning down consciousness beyond this what-it's-likeness is very difficult. The second issue is that it is contentious whether consciousness is a necessary condition for having a mind. If we came across an organism which seemed to meet the above requirements but which we also believed was not conscious, then would we be justified in denying that organism a mind? Is it even possible to have a creature which had thoughts about things but which was not conscious? These are important and still very much debated questions. The ephemeral nature of consciousness is such that, like Winnie-the-Pooh's quarry, we're not entirely sure what it is we're looking for until we catch up with it.

Cartesian dualism

We will now track some of the twists and turns philosophers have taken in trying to answer *the Question* (that is, what it is to have a mind) which will help us understand how some philosophers came to the idea that the mind is a kind of computer. We begin with Cartesian dualism, the view briefly presented in the introduction, which maintains that our minds are made from a fundamentally different substance to that of our bodies. This chimes with lots of our intuitions about our minds: the view that our minds are importantly different from our bodies forms a central tenet in many world religions, and the thought that we are 'meat' through and through is, for many, an unsettling one. The mind, that part of us which thinks, loves and creates, seems so different from anything else in the world that it is not unreasonable to think that this is because it is made of something entirely different.

There are several arguments that Descartes offers in support of this view, the most important of which can be found in the *Meditations* (1641). I will focus on the 'argument from doubt' found in the Second Meditation. There is some disagreement among specialists on Descartes' work about how to interpret this argument, but what I present here is a common reading. It looks like this:

Premise 1. I can doubt the existence of my body.
Premise 2. I cannot doubt the existence of my thoughts (my mind).
Conclusion. Therefore, my mind must be made of something fundamentally different from everything else around me.

Descartes believed that his argument showed that the mind must be made of a different substance to that of his body and other things found in the physical world. This is because it has a property that physical things do not have: its existence cannot be doubted. To put it another way: I can imagine that the physical world does not exist, but it is impossible for me to imagine that I don't exist, because there has to be something which is doing the imagining! Hence the famous *Cogito*: 'I think therefore I am.' In order to think, there must be something which is doing the thinking, and that thing is my mind. Let's go through the argument examining each premise and whether they collectively logically support the conclusion.

Premise 1. I can doubt the existence of my body.

Descartes claims that he can imagine having no body at all while his mental life persists. Therefore, having a mind must be distinct from having a body because we can imagine one existing without the other.

Premise 2. I cannot doubt the existence of my thoughts.

While it may be the case that I can doubt that the world around me exists, I can't doubt that I am thinking. Thoughts, by their very nature, belong to someone. Thoughts can't drift around 'unowned'. In order for there to be thoughts, there has to be someone who is doing the thinking. And, in order for there to be doubts, there must be someone who is doing the doubting. Therefore, although I can doubt that the world exists, I cannot doubt that whatever it is that is doing the doubting, exists. In this instance, the thing that is doing the doubting is surely me. So, while I can doubt the existence of everything around me, I cannot doubt the existence of my own mind, because my mind has to exist in order for any doubting to occur.

Conclusion. Therefore, my mind must be made of something fundamentally different from everything else around me.

This conclusion draws on **Leibniz's law,** so called after the philosopher who posited it, Gottfried Leibniz (1646–1716). Leibniz's law states that two things are identical (one and the same) if and only if they share all the same properties. Two snooker balls share the properties of being red, having a circumference of 52.5 millimetres, and weighing 142 grams. However, they do not share the same spatial properties, as they occupy different places on the baize, so the snooker balls are not one and the same thing. By contrast, Ronnie O'Sullivan and 'the 2013 World Snooker Champion' share all the same properties, and thus Ronnie O'Sullivan is identical with the 2013 World Snooker Champion.

All this matters because Descartes is arguing against the claim that the mind and the body are one and the same thing. If the mind and the body are one and the same thing then they must share all the same properties. But the mind and the body do not share all the same properties because one can doubt the existence of the body (premise 1) but one cannot doubt the existence of the mind (premise 2). Therefore, by Leibniz's law, the mind and the body cannot be one and the same thing, because they differ in their properties.

A challenge to the argument from doubt

The most pressing problem with the argument from doubt is that, while revealing about the nature of doubt, the argument sheds little light on the nature of the mind. This point was made by Leibniz in his *Philosophical Papers*, and by Antoine Arnauld, a contemporary of Descartes. An example helps illustrate the point.

Let's imagine that I am unaware that Dr Jekyll is Mr Hyde. I can imagine a scenario where Dr Jekyll apprehends Mr Hyde and leaves him in the custody of the police, going home to a warm supper while Mr Hyde languishes in his cell cursing Jekyll. Yet this imagining does not inform me of what is in fact possible. Rather, it reveals a limitation on my knowledge which cannot be appreciated from my current perspective. It is generally correct to state that if two things have different properties then those two things are distinct. But this doesn't hold once we throw psychological terms in there, because my beliefs might not map on to how the world actually is. I believe that Dr Jekyll has the property of being kind, and I believe that Mr Hyde lacks this property (being a murdering psychopath), and I infer from these beliefs that because Dr Jekyll has a property that Mr Hyde lacks, they must be distinct people. This believing, however, does not preclude the possibility that they are identical. Thus, where psychological verbs like believe, imagine, think, etc., are concerned, Leibniz's law may mislead us. It may be the case that I can doubt the existence of my body and I cannot doubt the existence of my mind, but as the example of Jekyll and Hyde shows, such doubting is not enough to show that the two are distinct.

A challenge to Cartesian dualism

We have seen that the argument from doubt does not support Cartesian dualism. However, the failure of one argument does not necessarily undermine a view and Cartesian dualism might still be true even if the argument from doubt fails. We now turn to an argument which specifically challenges the *dualism* in Cartesian dualism. This is the argument from causation, and it was first proposed by one of Descartes' brightest students, Princess Elisabeth of Bohemia (1618–80).

In 1643, the Princess wrote to Descartes asking him to explain how the mind is able to interact with the body if they are made of fundamentally distinct substances. In other words, the Princess was challenging Cartesian dualism on the grounds of our first requirement in the second section (pp. 38–9): how can Cartesian dualism explain mental causation, from the mind to the body and from the body to the mind? Substances of different kinds do not seem able to causally interact: it is not clear how a substance which isn't located in space can interact with one that is. Our knowledge of the physical world suggests that the only interactions that are possible are those between physical bodies. The Cartesian dualist is required to either give an account of how the immaterial can interact with the material or to deny that such interaction occurs. As previously observed, denying mental–physical interaction leads to a view of the mind that is so alien one is entitled to say that it isn't actually an account of the mind. Causation is one of our key requirements in our answer to *the Question*, and thus the onus is on the Cartesian dualist to give an account of how two different substances can interact. However, a plausible account has yet to be given.

The identity theory

The sticking point for Cartesian dualism is that it posits two kinds of substance: immaterial and material stuff. What happens if we drop the dualism and simply say that there is only one kind of substance in the world, and that is material substance? (Of course, one could choose to say that the only kind of substance in the world is immaterial, as was argued by George Berkeley (1685–1753).) Material substance occupies a certain amount of space, and everything that exists can be explained by talking about relations between different types of material substance. A contemporary articulation of this view is **physicalism,** the view that everything which exists can be explained by physics. The mind is no exception: we don't need to appeal to strange substances whose behaviour cannot be accommodated by physics in order to explain it. Although modern physics posits massless entities which might be understood as immaterial in a Cartesian sense an exploration of how philosophers should understand 'physical' in the light of modern physics is beyond the scope of this chapter. In this section we examine a physicalist view known as the **identity theory**.

The identity theory is the view that our mental states are identical with physical states. The example most loved by philosophers is that the mental state of pain is identical with the activity of C-fibres. (Clearly the neurological basis of pain is more complex than the activity of one particular collection of neural fibres, but this short cut will do for our purposes.) A big advantage of the view is that it can address the causation requirement set out earlier. The identity theory cheerfully accepts that everything which exists is material, and thus interaction between the mind and the body is possible. When I have the desire for cake (in conjunction with other mental states) the mix of chemicals which this state is identical with transfers energy along my nervous system to my arm, causing it to reach out for the cake. We don't need to posit anything beyond the realms of the physical sciences in order to explain how our thoughts can cause our actions. There are several different ways of understanding the identity relation between mental states and physical states which we won't go into here, but which can be explored further in some of the books mentioned in the further reading sections.

Functionalism

Hilary Putnam, in his 1967 paper 'The Nature of Mental States', raised an important objection to the identity theory. Imagine that we find the cocktail of chemicals which we are certain is identical to the mental state of feeling pain. Putnam says that all we've done is find out the identity relation between pain and its physical realization *in humans*. Let's assume, for the sake of argument, that octopus brains are made up of totally different chemicals to those of human brains but that we have good reason to believe that these critters feel pain, e.g. they withdraw from hot stimuli, they engage in avoidance behaviour around those stimuli, we see a spike in their brain activity when they touch hot things. Do we want to deny them pain because their brains are made up of different stuff to ours? Of course not, says Putnam.

Multiple realizability

The key point for Putnam is that mental states are **multiply realizable**. Lots of things are multiply realizable. Chairs are a good example. If I want a new chair for my office I could open my internet browser and type 'chair' into the search engine. The result will show thousands of different types of chair: wooden chairs, plastic chairs, rocking chairs, polka-dot chairs, chairs with four distinct legs and chairs carved out of giant cubes. What allows us to say that all these things are instances of chairs is that they share a common function: they facilitate sitting. An object which did not have this function, e.g. a plank of wood, could not rightly be called a chair, even if it consisted of material that chairs are sometimes made from. Chairs are therefore multiply realizable: there are lots of different materials that could 'realize' a chair.

The claim that mental states are multiply realizable just means that any mental state, e.g. the mental state of wanting a pet llama, can be instantiated in a variety of different physical systems. A system made out of H_2O and other chemicals (like us) could feasibly want a pet llama; alternatively, an alien with a very different physiological make-up could also want a pet llama. We don't want to say that aliens can't have mental states just because their brains are made of different stuff to ours. There might be other reasons that we have for saying they don't have minds, e.g. their behaviour doesn't match that which we'd expect from a minded being, but it would be unreasonable to decree that they can't have minds just because they don't share the same biology as ourselves.

Putnam's insight had a significant impact on contemporary **philosophy of mind**. He was saying that rather than thinking about mental phenomena in terms of what they might be made of physically (because this leads to all sorts of problems when it comes to non-humans) we should be thinking about them in terms of what they *do*. This led to the **functionalist** account of mental states. Functionalists claim that trying to give an account of mental states in terms of what they're made of is like trying to explain what a chair is in terms of what it's made of. What makes something a chair is whether that thing can *function* as a chair: can it support you sitting on it? Does it have support for your back? Does it raise your sitting position up from the ground? Chairs can be made of lots of different things, and look completely different, but what makes them identifiable as chairs is the job that they do.

Putnam's big claim was that we should identify mental states not by what they're made of, but by what they do. And the function of mental states is to be caused by sensory stimuli and prior mental states, and to cause behaviour and new mental states. The belief that tigers are dangerous is distinct from the desire to hug a tiger in virtue of what that belief does (Figure 3.1). The desire to hug a tiger would cause me to rush towards the tiger with open arms, and it might be caused by the belief that tigers are harmless human-loving creatures. Whereas the belief that tigers are dangerous is caused by my previous knowledge that tigers occasionally eat people and that creatures with big teeth are dangerous, and serves to cause running away behaviour as well as new

Figure 3.1 Mental causation in seeing a tiger.

mental states such as dislike of the person who let the tiger into the room in the first place. To make the contrast with the identity theory clearer: according to the identity theory what makes the *belief that tigers are dangerous* distinct from *the desire to hug a tiger* is the different chemical cocktails which those states consist in. But functionalists say that this is wrong: what makes each of these states distinct is their different functional roles. They might also be made of different chemicals, but that's by the by. The interesting difference lies in what causes them and what they do.

Pause for thought

Let's not lose sight of *the Question*. We are interested in what a mind is. So far we have ascertained that a mind probably isn't an immaterial thing. It is probably made of the same kinds of material as everything else in the world, and as such can be explained by appeal to the same physical laws that govern everything else in the world. As a consequence, we ditched dualism in favour of views that don't posit any extra, immaterial, stuff. The first of the physicalist views that we examined was the identity theory. The identity theory looked promising: although there are nuances in how one spells out the idea of identity the general idea that mental states are identical with brain states is appealing. After all, we are always hearing about discoveries made using fMRI scans of the brain and how are we to make sense of these without the identity theory? Furthermore, the identity theory appears to meet one of our main requirements for an account of the mind because it can explain how mental states can effect bodily changes. Things are looking good.

But how, exactly, does the identity theory help with *the Question*? What is it to have a mind, on this view? It looks like the identity theory has to say that having a mind is to be in some kind of physical state, e.g. having particular neurons active, and this is identical to being in a particular mental state. So, having a mind is just a question of having neurons firing in the right way. This doesn't seem right, though, because we don't want to rule out creatures whose physical make-up is very different from ours from having a mind.

One way around this problem is to be more specific: in humans, having a mind requires having neurons that are active in a particular way; in octopuses, it is having neurons that fire in a different way; and in aliens from the planet Zoog, it is having alien goo that slops around in a particular sort of way. Each organism has its own biological requirements for having a mind.

It was at this point we moved to our second account, namely, functionalism. Functionalism says that we identify minds by what they do. (As a consequence, the functionalist is agnostic regarding whether minds are made of immaterial or material stuff, although it should be noted that the majority of functionalist views are physicalist ones.) Mental states are internal states that change in accordance with stimulation received from our senses and other internal states that we happen to be in. If I am in the state of hunger (which has been caused by sensory signals from my stomach) and I perceive a cake, then I will switch to an inner state of happiness and engage in the behaviour of reaching for, and eating, the cake. Clearly this is an oversimplification of the function of each mental state: there will be millions of different combinations that could come about depending on the sensory input, as well as an indefinite number of new mental states that could arise from the combination of two or more current states. I might want a llama, I might believe that keeping a llama in my flat will anger my landlady, and I want to avoid antagonizing my landlady. Together these states function to cause me to think that maybe I can compromise by adopting a local llama, or persuading my friends who own a house to buy a llama.

This brings us to the second part of the chapter. As I mentioned in the introduction philosophers and psychologists often talk about the mind as if it were a computer. Now that functionalism is on the table we can begin to appreciate the reason for this. Computers are information-processing machines: they take information of one kind, e.g. an electrical pulse caused by the depression of a key, and turn it into information of another kind, e.g. a number displayed on a screen. Furthermore, what makes a computer a computer is not what it is made out of, but whether it can process information. On a functionalist view our minds are also information-processing machines: they take information provided by our senses and other mental states which we have, process it, and produce new behaviours and mental states. We individuate mental states by processes which require certain starting conditions (particular mental states and sensations) and result in end conditions in the form of new mental states and behaviours. The similarity goes further: what allows us to identify something as a computer or a mind is what that thing does, and not what it is made of. Computers come in varying degrees of complexity. There is a computer in my washing machine that controls the various cycles. There are also computers that can generate complex probabilistic models which we use to predict all kinds of phenomena: weather cycles, biological degradation, wave formations, etc. If we accept that minds are computing machines, then how complex does an information-processing system need to be for it to count as a mind? This is the question we address in the next section.

The imitation game

In his landmark paper 'Computing Machinery and Intelligence' (1950) Alan Turing (1912–54) proposed the 'imitation game', a potential experiment which could help philosophers and others address the question of whether machines can think. Turing asks us to imagine three people – a questioner, a male respondent and a female respondent – who are asked to play an 'imitation game'. The questioner is in a different room to the respondents and can communicate with them via an instant messenger style set-up: the questioner types questions which appear on screens in front of the responding man and woman, who in turn can type messages back. The task set to the questioner is to determine which of the respondents, labelled only as X and Y, is the man, and which is the woman. The man's task is to mislead the questioner into believing that he is the woman and the woman's task is to help the questioner make the right identification.

The next stage of the game is very similar, except that one of the respondents is replaced by a computer, and the questioner's task is to determine which of the respondents is the human and which is the computer. The computer's task is to mislead the questioner into believing it is the human and the human respondent's task is to help the questioner. What would happen, asked Turing, if the computer could trick the questioner as often, when the game is played in this way, as another human is able to trick the questioner when it is played with a man and a woman? One possible answer to this question – and the one Turing seemed drawn to – is that if a computer can consistently fool the interrogator into believing that it is a human then the computer has reached the level of functional complexity required for having a mind.

How should we evaluate this answer? It might be possible that a machine with an extremely large database and a powerful search engine passes the test (this possibility is raised by Jaegwon Kim (2006)). Thus, when asked what 84 – 13 is, the machine whizzes to its set of files labelled 'possible subtraction sums', pulls out the file labelled '84 – 13' (perhaps it is nestled between the files labelled '84 – 14' and '84 – 12') and displays whatever it finds in that file. And it does the same for questions like 'do you prefer your martinis shaken or stirred?' or 'what are your views on Tarantino films?' A machine which simply had all the answers in storage and a sensitive and powerful search engine does not seem to qualify as a 'thinking machine', because it does not have the internal structure we expect of a minded thing. This counterexample is intended to show that the internal structure of a processing machine matters when it comes to determining whether it is minded, and therefore a machine that passes the test should not immediately be classified as minded. It leaves open the question of what kind of internal structure we should expect a minded thing to have.

It is important to point out that Turing's aim in introducing the game was to provide a more focused question than the generic 'Can machines think?' This question seems too vague to found a research programme, whereas 'Can a machine trick us into thinking that it is human?' is more tractable. The imitation game was intended to steer our thoughts in the right direction for answering larger questions concerning machine thought, or thought more generally. It serves as a useful signpost in our quest to answer *the Question*, but passing the test does not guarantee mindedness, because it does not take into account the internal organization of the machine.

Searle's Chinese room

The idea that the mind is a computing machine is a powerful one. However, there are problems with the view, and I'd like to point to some of these using John Searle's Chinese room thought experiment (1980). Searle asks us to imagine the following situation. You are in a sealed room, the walls of which are lined with books containing Chinese symbols. For the sake of the experiment we shall assume that you do not understand any Chinese at all. In fact, you are so ignorant of Chinese that you do not even know that the patterns in the books are linguistic symbols. There is a slot in the door through which pieces of paper with patterns on them are posted. You have a code book which contains a set of rules (written in English) that tells you what to do when particular patterns are posted through the slot; usually this means going to one of the books in the library, opening it to a particular page, copying the pattern you see there onto the piece of paper you have received, and posting it back out through the slot. The code book covers all possible combinations of patterns that you might receive.

Now let's suppose that outside of the room is a native speaker of Chinese. Unbeknown to you, she is posting questions in Chinese through the slot and you are giving her coherent answers to these questions. Although she believes that she is conversing with someone who understands Chinese, you actually do not understand any Chinese at all, you don't even know that you are engaged in a communicative act!

Clearly this situation is rather far-fetched and Searle wasn't aiming to persuade us that it is at all plausible. His aim was to use the thought experiment to probe our intuitions about mindedness by pointing to a fundamental issue facing the view that the mind is a computing machine. Computers work by processing symbols. Symbols have **syntactic** and **semantic** properties (Figure 3.2). Their syntactic properties are their *geometric* properties, e.g. shape. 'Syntax' also refers to the set of rules by which these symbols can be manipulated in accordance with their shape. Their semantic property is what they mean, or what they stand for.

Computers, calculators and other symbol-manipulating machines are only sensitive to the syntactic properties of symbols. We program machines with rules that operate on the syntactic structure of the symbols it receives. For example, we can program a computer with a rule such that if it receives the input of a circle followed by the input of a triangle then it should produce the output of a triangle in a circle. The computer can do this operation just by 'looking' at the physical structure of the shapes.

Searle observed that the computer does not 'know' that it is manipulating symbols that have semantic content any more than the person

Figure 3.2 The properties of symbols. This sign is commonly used to mean 'No Entry'. It has the *syntactic* properties of being a red circle with a white rectangle in the middle of it. Its *semantic* property is that it stands for the instruction, 'do not enter'.

inside Searle's Chinese room knows she is manipulating Chinese characters. One can give an exhaustive description of a computational system by describing how the arrangement of symbols changes in a rule-governed way according to their shapes. This leads to a fundamental issue with the claim that the mind is a computing machine: what part of the machine understands the symbols that it is manipulating? With a computer it doesn't matter that the machine's processing has nothing to do with the semantic content of the symbols because it is the humans who use the machine that have this information: we are the ones who give meaning to those symbols. Searle concludes that a computational theory of mind fails to explain how our mental states have meaning or 'aboutness', causing it to fail our second requirement of an account of what it is to have a mind. Minds have a feature which computers do not have: computers do not have 'aboutness', they do not have an understanding of what the symbols they manipulate stand for. If minds have a feature which computers do not have, then the claim that our minds are computing machines fails.

Searle's second consideration, which he discusses in his 1998 book *The Mystery of Consciousness*, concerns the representational nature of symbols. Symbols are a type of representation because they stand for something. Other forms of representation include portraits or statues. But what makes something a representation? What makes something a representation is whether it functions in a particular way. Like mental states and chairs, we pick out representational things not by what they are made of but by what they do. Importantly, for our purposes, 'to represent' is a three-place verb: x represents y to z. When I'm at the pub I can use beer mats and beer mugs to represent my position on the football field to my friends by saying 'This mug is me, this mat is the defender and that crisp packet is the goal.' The *mug* represents *my position on the football field* to *my friends and me*.

In order for anything to be a representation, there must be someone who takes it to be a representation. The beer mug sitting on the table is not a representation until I treat it as one. Computing fundamentally involves the manipulation of symbols, and so in order for any process to count as a computational one there must be someone who treats these symbols *as symbols* and in doing so is able to understand the process as a computational one. In order for a process to count as a computational one there must be someone who interprets it as being such. In the case of the computer we decide what each symbol should stand for, and as a consequence we can recognize the changes in the physical state of a computer as a computational process because we recognise it as manipulating symbols. In the case of the mind we are left with a puzzle: the activation of neuron 345 represents a dog *to whom*? Who is it that confers representational status to the physical states of the mind, and in doing so is able to see the changes between these physical states as a computational process? In order for something to be a computational process there must be someone who treats it as one. But in the case of our thoughts, it's not clear who that someone is.

Understanding the mind as a computer allows us to address our causation requirement for an account of the mind, but it fails to address the 'aboutness' requirement. Should we, therefore, stop describing minds as computers? Does Searle's Chinese room thought experiment damage the computational account of the mind as much as Princess Elisabeth's causation challenge damaged Cartesian dualism? There are considerably more philosophers trying to defend the computational view of the mind than there are those trying to defend Cartesian dualism; they believe the answer to this question is 'no'. However, Searle's thought experiment serves as a healthy warning to those who accept too readily the claim that the mind is a computer, challenging them to think about how, exactly, the parallels should be drawn.

The extended mind

We have looked at how functionalism influenced a school of thought which maintains that minds are computers. To end this chapter, we turn to another contemporary area of research that has its roots in functionalism, called the **extended mind hypothesis**.

'The Extended Mind' is the title of a 1998 paper by Andy Clark and David Chalmers, which explores the consequences of the multiple realizability aspect of functionalism. A brief reminder: because functionalism maintains that we should identify mental states by what they do rather than by what the minded individual is made of, functionalism accepts that individuals made of very different kinds of material could all nonetheless possess minds. Clark and Chalmers take this a step further to suggest that mental states might not even be located in our heads, illustrating their claim with the following thought experiment (p. 12). Two people, Otto and Inga, want to see an exhibition at the Museum of Modern Art. Inga thinks briefly about where the Museum of Modern Art is, recalls that it is on 53rd Street, and walks to 53rd Street and into the museum. Otto has a form of Alzheimer's disease and to cope with the effect this has on his memory he writes information down in a notebook which he carries wherever he goes. When he learns something new he logs it in his notebook, and when he needs to access old information he looks it up. When Otto wants to go to the exhibition he looks at his notebook and sees that the museum is on 53rd Street, and off he goes to the museum.

Clark and Chalmers claim that Otto's notebook plays the same functional role for him as Inga's biological memory does for her. In order to see this, we need to examine briefly a distinction philosophers make between **occurrent** and **non-occurrent** beliefs. We all have beliefs that we are not currently aware of. I believe that Edinburgh is the capital city of Scotland and it is fair to say that I have that belief even if I am not currently thinking about it. If I am thinking about something else (e.g. concentrating on cooking a cheese soufflé) or asleep we don't want to say that I no longer believe that Edinburgh is the capital city of Scotland simply because I am not currently aware of that belief. A belief is occurrent when you are aware of it, or are thinking about it; a belief is non-occurrent when you have that belief but you are not currently aware of it or thinking about it. Other mental states, like desires and hopes, can also be occurrent or non-occurrent.

This matters because Clark and Chalmers claim that, prior to hearing about the exhibition and forming the desire to go to it, both Otto and Inga have the non-occurrent belief that the museum is on 53rd Street. When this belief becomes occurrent it functions in exactly the same way in both of them: when paired with the 'desire to go to the museum' it causes 'walking to 53rd Street' behaviour. We can explain both Inga's and Otto's behaviour by appeal to their occurrent belief about where the museum is, their occurrent desire to go to the museum, and the fact that they each had this belief prior to thinking about it, i.e. they each had a non-occurrent belief about the location of the museum. The only difference is that when Inga's belief about the museum is non-occurrent it is stored in her biological memory, and when Otto's belief about the museum is non-occurrent it is stored in his notebook. However, the beliefs are functionally identical: they both cause the same behaviour when they are occurrent and paired with a particular desire.

Otto's belief is extended because it is partly constituted by an artefact beyond his head, namely, his notebook. If something damages Otto's notebook then he no longer has a non-occurrent belief about the location of the museum and will therefore be unable to form an occurrent belief about its location. Otto's non-occurrent belief about the museum's location is realized by the information in the notebook coupled with Otto and his dispositions to interact with, and be guided by, that information in particular ways. As a consequence, we can say that Otto's belief about the museum's location is partly constituted by the notebook, and therefore a part of what constitutes Otto's belief is located outside of Otto's head.

When Putnam introduced the idea of mental states being multiply realizable he did so because he thought that we shouldn't limit mentality to creatures with a specific physical make-up. Clark and Chalmers' project is very similar. However, their claim is that we should not limit mentality to only those processes that go on in our heads. This is an arbitrary limitation, as arbitrary as saying that only creatures with the same biological make-up as humans can have thoughts. They argue that a process which is distributed between an organism and some artefact in the world (such as Otto and his notebook) deserves to be called a cognitive process if it is the case that, were that process contained entirely in the head (like Inga retrieving information from her biological memory), we would have no hesitation in calling it cognitive.

The extended mind hypothesis has completely shaken philosophers' preconceptions of what it is to have a mind. In particular, it has opened up a huge debate about where the limits of the mind are. If mental states like beliefs can extend beyond the body, then how far can they extend? The hypothesis has also shaped a new movement known as 'embodied cognition', the view that our bodies as well as our brains can constitute part of the cognitive process. If the extended mind hypothesis is true, then it looks like our answer to the question of what it is to have a mind will involve our bodies and the world in ways that we are only just beginning to understand.

Where are we now?

The first part of this chapter looked at different theories of mind ending with functionalism. In the second part we examined two significant developments which are grounded in functionalism: the theory that minds are computers, and the theory that minds extend beyond our heads. Functionalism has certainly made an impact on the philosophy of mind! It is perhaps worth remembering that functionalism, along with the view that minds are computers, appeared on the philosophical scene at a time when the potential of computing machines dominated scientific and public imaginations. Theories are often influenced by the dominant technologies of their time, and one might worry that this happened with philosophy of mind in the latter part of the twentieth century. John Searle successfully cautions against the temptation to assume that the mind is a computer by observing that minds have a feature which computers do not, namely, 'aboutness'. Furthermore, as he also notes, a process only counts as a computational one relative to an observer and it is not at all clear who the observer is in the case of the mind.

Finally, we looked at the claim that if functionalism is true then mental states might extend into the world. This is a natural consequence of the multiple realizability aspect of functionalism: if a mental state can be made of different materials, then why can't we also say that some of the materials that constitute a mental state exist outside of the head? If Otto's notebook plays the same functional role for him as Inga's biological memory does for her, then Otto's notebook is a constituent of his mental state of 'believing the museum is on 53rd Street'. This means that our mental states need not all be contained in our head, and that some of them might extend into the world. The extended mind and its consequences are among the hottest topics in current philosophy of mind, causing philosophers to completely rethink how we should go about answering the question of what it is to have a mind.

Chapter summary

- An account of what it is to have a mind must accommodate two things: (a) how our minds can cause changes in our bodies, and how changes in our bodies can cause changes to our minds; and (b) how our thoughts can be about things.
- René Descartes thought that the mind is distinct from the body. This view is Cartesian dualism.
- Descartes' main argument for this view – the argument from doubt – does not work.
- Cartesian dualism also cannot explain our first criterion for what an account of the mind should do: it cannot explain the causal relations that exist between our minds and our bodies.
- Physicalism is the view that everything that exists is physical, and as such can solve the problem of causation.
- The identity theory is a physicalist view which claims that mental states are identical to (one and the same as) physical brain states.
- Functionalism is the view that something counts as a mind if it functions like one, and we should not be concerned with what a mind is made of.
- Turing's imitation game accepts functionalism, and tests the hypothesis that something functions as a mind if it can trick another person into believing that it is minded.
- One way of developing functionalism is to say that minds are computers, because like computers their function is to process information.

- Searle's Chinese room argument challenges the claim that minds are computers by showing us that (a) this view is unable to address how thoughts can be about things, and (b) that in order for a process to be computational, there must be someone who interprets it as being so. There is no such person in the case of the mind.
- The extended mind hypothesis builds on functionalism to show that mental states need not be located in our heads. Instead, they can extend out into the world.

Study questions

1 Can you think of some other arguments in favour of Cartesian dualism? In the light of Princess Elisabeth's challenge, it's very easy to see why the view might be wrong. It's more challenging – and good philosophical exercise – to try to think of reasons for it!
2 Can the identity theory work? If brain states are not identical with mental states, then how should we make sense of brain scans that purport to show the brain activity underlying a particular mental state?
3 Do you agree with the functionalist's principle that we should identify mental states by what they do, rather than by what they're made of? Can you think of reasons for disagreeing with this claim?
4 If a computer can pass Turing's imitation game, does it have a mind?
5 How should we understand the concept of a 'representation'?
6 What are Searle's reasons for denying that the mind is a computer?
7 Can you think of examples of mental processes which extend into the world? When do you think a process ceases to be a cognitive one?

Introductory further reading

Blackmore, S. (2005) *Conversations on Consciousness*, Oxford: Oxford University Press. (The psychologist Susan Blackmore interviews philosophers (including John Searle), neuroscientists and psychologists about, you've guessed it, consciousness. A fascinating read which maintains an informal tone while being very informative.)

Crane, T. (1995) *The Mechanical Mind*, London: Penguin. (A beautifully written and accessible introduction to the issues discussed in this chapter, and especially clear on the problem of 'aboutness'.)

Advanced further reading

Clark, A. (2008) *Supersizing the Mind*, Oxford: Oxford University Press. (A detailed exploration of the extended mind hypothesis.)

Clark, A. and Chalmers, D. (1998) 'The Extended Mind,' *Analysis* 58: 7–19; also available from *CogPrints* (see below). (The first statement of the extended mind hypothesis, and includes the now famous Otto and Inga case. It is currently the most cited paper from the journal *Analysis*.)

Descartes, R. (1641/1996) *Meditations on First Philosophy*, trans. J. Cottingham, with an introduction by B. Williams, Cambridge: Cambridge University Press, 1996. (Original source of Cartesian dualism and seminal work in philosophy. This and many other translations are available.)

Hofstadter, D. and Dennett, D. D. (eds) (1981) *The Mind's I: Fantasies and Reflections on Self and Soul*, New York: Basic Books. (A lovely collection of readings (including Turing's 'Computing Machinery and Intelligence', and Nagel's 'What Is It Like to Be a Bat') with thought-provoking and entertaining commentary by the editors.)

Kim, J. (2006) *The Philosophy of Mind*, Boulder, CO: Westview. (There are two editions of this book, both are excellent. This is the place to go to find out more about the different types of identity theory.)

Searle, J. (1980) 'Minds, Brains and Programs,' *Behavioral and Brain Sciences* 3: 417–24. (This is the paper that introduces the Chinese room thought experiment.)

——(1998) *The Mystery of Consciousness*, London: Granta. (Here you can find Searle's critique of the 'minds are computers' claim, and a philosophical exploration of consciousness.)

Smith, P. and Jones, O. R. (1986) *The Philosophy of Mind*, Cambridge: Cambridge University Press. (I have yet to find a more rigorous and accessible examination of Cartesian dualism and its problems (chs 1–5).)

Turing, A. (1950) 'Computing Machinery and Intelligence,' *Mind* 59: 433–60. (There are lots of free versions of the paper available online, and it pops up in lots of philosophy of mind anthologies (e.g. the Hofstadter and Dennett above). I'd suggest omitting sections 4 and 5 on the first reading.)

Internet resources

CogPrints: Cognitive Sciences Eprint Archive [website], http://cogprints.org/view/subjects/phil-mind.html. (A free collection of philosophy of mind papers, which includes the Turing (1950), Searle (1980), and Clark and Chalmers (1998) listed above.)

Some Texts from Early Modern Philosophy, ed. Jonathan F. Bennett [website], www.earlymoderntexts.com/de. (This is a great resource where philosophical texts have been annotated and reproduced using contemporary language. Descartes' *Meditations* can be found here.)

'Dan Dennett: The Illusion of Consciousness,' *TED: Ideas Worth Spreading* [website], April 2007 (filmed 2003), www.ted.com/talks/dan_dennett_on_our_consciousness.html. (The philosopher Daniel Dennett talks to us about the 'illusion' of consciousness.)

'Mirror Neurons', *The Headspace* [blog], www.mixcloud.com/headspaceradio/mirror-neurons. (My research interests extend beyond traditional problems in the philosophy of mind to the issue of how evidence from neuroscience and psychology should inform philosophical problems. If you're interested in hearing more about what I've been working on recently, you can hear an interview here.)

Films

Bladerunner (1982) Dir. Ridley Scott. (Spot the Turing test!)
Freaky Friday (1976) Dir. Gary Nelson or (2003) dir. Mark Waters (A mother and her teenage daughter swap bodies and experience the 'what-it's-likeness' of each other's lives. I won't lie, I like the 2003 one best.)
Memento (2000) Dir. Christopher Nolan (The hero's tattoos and notes function as his memory. Are they his extended mind?)
The Matrix (1999) Dir. Andy Wachowski and Lana Wachowski (A cinematic exploration of the argument from doubt and related themes.)

4   Morality

Objective, relative or emotive?

Matthew Chrisman

Introduction

In our everyday lives we make **moral judgments**, i.e. thoughts we might
express with statements like 'What you did was very kind', 'Pol Pot was
an evil man' or 'We have a moral obligation to help those in need'.
Philosophers who work on **ethics** also make moral judgments, but often
somewhat more abstractly. They say things like 'An action is right just
in case it maximizes overall happiness', or 'One ought to always act for
reasons that one could consistently allow everyone else to act for as
well'. This chapter is about the status of these judgments and the distinctively human practice of which they are a part. That is, it's about
the **status of morality**.

This is not a question of whether particular moral judgments, whether
everyday or abstract, are correct. Rather, it's about what we're doing
when we make moral judgments. Are our moral judgments attempts to
represent objective matters of fact? Or, are they implicitly relative
to our particular cultural situation? Do our moral statements attempt
to track features of the world around us? Or, do they express emotive
reactions to the value-free world as we take it to be? Nevertheless, for
the sake of concreteness I will use some examples of moral judgments,
and I have purposefully chosen examples that are somewhat controversial. This is not because I want to endorse (or deny) these moral
judgments here but because I hope their controversial nature helps you
to see the importance and difficulty in understanding the status of
morality.

First, we'll explore the question about the status of morality in a
little more detail, in order to try to understand what is being asked and
why it is fundamental for the philosophical study of ethics. Then, we'll
learn about three basic approaches philosophers have taken to the
issue: **objectivism**, **relativism** and **emotivism**. Next, we'll briefly consider

some of the advantages and disadvantages of each approach, with the hope of helping you to start thinking about which kind of view you might favour and how you might argue for it. Finally, I'll seek to point you in the direction of further things to think about and read regarding the status of morality.

The status of morality: what's the issue?

In order to get our heads around the topic of this chapter, it'll be helpful to generate and think about two lists. First we'll want a list of **empirical judgments** about the way things are in the world around us. For example, in the sixteenth and seventeenth centuries, Copernicus, Kepler and Galileo all helped us to understand that the Earth rotates around the sun. In the eighteenth century, Benjamin Franklin discovered that there are positive and negative electrical charges. In the nineteenth century, Mendel explained how some traits in plants are passed on to offspring according to laws of inheritance, based on dominant and recessive genes. And in the twenty-first century, scientists at CERN (the European Laboratory for Particle Physics) in Switzerland confirmed that the Higgs boson particle (aka 'the God particle') exists. However, when I say that we want a list of empirical judgments about the way things are in the world around us, I don't mean to limit us to statements of grand scientific discovery. More mundane examples will also work, such as the claim that lead is heavier than iron, or that it was sunny in Edinburgh today (13 May 2013), or even that I (Matthew Chrisman) am less than six feet tall. OK, that'll do for our first list.

Next we'll want a list of moral judgments about what's morally right/wrong, good/bad, etc. Let's start with some positive claims, such as that giving to charity is morally praiseworthy, it's good to take care of your children, and non-violently protesting something you take to be a gross injustice is morally justifiable. Now add to that some negative claims, such as that Cain's murdering Abel was morally wrong, or that Oedipus sleeping with his mother Jocasta was morally bad. Similarly, someone might say that the actions of Pol Pot and the Khmer Rouge during the Cambodian Genocide were morally abhorrent, or that the practice of polygamy – having multiple wives (or husbands) – is morally dubious.

Here these are, somewhat abbreviated, in list form:

Empirical judgments
The Earth rotates around the sun.
Electricity has positive and negative charges.

Plant traits can be genetically inherited.
The Higgs boson particle exists.
Lead is heavier than iron.
It was sunny in Edinburgh on 13 May 2013.
Matthew Chrisman is less than six feet tall.

Moral judgments
Giving to charity is morally praiseworthy.
It's good to take care of your children.
Cain's murdering Abel was morally wrong.
Oedipus' sleeping with Jocasta was morally bad.
Protesting injustice is morally justifiable.
The actions of Pol Pot were morally abhorrent.
Polygamy is morally dubious.

Some of the statements on these lists might be controversial, or might have been controversial at some earlier stage in history. It's not really important which particular empirical and moral judgments we consider but that we consider examples that fall clearly into one or the other category. I encourage you to come up with some more examples of your own. Once you have your own lists of empirical judgments and of moral judgments (or if you're using my list), now we will ask three questions about the items on these two lists:

(A) Are they the sort of thing that can be true or false, or are they 'mere' opinion?
(B) If they can be true or false, what makes them true when they are true?
(C) If they are true, are they objectively true?

These questions are not empirical or moral questions; they are questions about the *status* of empirical and moral judgments.

The reason for considering these two lists is that many philosophers have had the intuition that morality is importantly different from empirical discovery and observation when it comes to these questions about its status. For example, it's quite natural to think that my judgments expressed in the following statements are the sorts of things that can be true or false:

(1) The Earth rotates around the sun.
(2) It was sunny in Edinburgh on 13 May 2013.

Indeed, (1) and (2) are true and seem to be objectively true. By contrast, some philosophers have suggested that moral judgments like those expressed in the following statements are not the sorts of judgments that can be true or false – not really:

(3) Polygamy is morally dubious.
(4) Oedipus' sleeping with Jocasta was morally bad.

These philosophers argue that (3) and (4) express 'mere' opinions. The basic idea is that they express our moral attitudes rather than beliefs about the way the world is.

Other philosophers have disagreed, but they too sense a difference between moral judgments and empirical judgments; they say that moral judgments are not objectively true or false, but only true or false relative to a system of morals or relative to someone's moral attitudes.

There is still another group of philosophers who deny both of these ideas and say that the truth or falsity of moral judgments like (3) and (4) is just as objective as the truth and falsity of empirical judgments like (1) and (2). That is, they think that the moral judgments expressed in our examples of moral statements aspire to the same kind of objectivity as the empirical judgments expressed in our examples of empirical statements.

This debate – the debate about questions like (A)–(C) about moral judgments – is about the status of morality. That's what we will explore in the rest of this chapter. I will explain three types of philosophical theories about the status of morality: objectivism, relativism and emotivism.

Objectivism

As I suggested before, one view we might take about the status of morality is that it is just as objective as the status of science. This view is sometimes called objectivism. The basic idea in objectivism is that our moral opinions are the sorts of things that can be true or false, and what makes them true or false are facts that are generally independent of who we are or what cultural groups we belong to – they are objective moral facts.

To get a feel for objectivism, consider again one of your examples of an empirical judgment about the world around us. My main examples have been the statements

(1) The Earth rotates around the sun.
(2) It was sunny in Edinburgh on 13 May 2013.

Let's ask questions (A)–(C) about the judgments expressed by (1) and (2).

I've already said that I think they are true. That is, if someone instead thought that the Earth does not rotate around the sun, or that it was not sunny in Edinburgh on 13 May 2012, such judgments would be false. Of course, not everyone throughout the course of history has thought that (1) is true. For a long time it was almost unheard of to think that the Earth rotates around the sun, rather than that the sun rotates around the Earth. And when scientists like Copernicus, Kepler and Galileo began to amass empirical evidence in favour of (1), their work was hugely controversial. Nevertheless, this seems to be a controversy about some objective matter of fact, and the controversy has been settled by better and better empirical observation and the improvement of our cosmological theory. Also, not everyone agrees about what it takes for it to count as 'sunny'; there are borderline cases. But assuming that there was an obvious period of clear bright sunshine in Edinburgh on that particular day, (2) is not a particularly controversial claim. So, the answer regarding (1) and (2) to question (A) is that these statements express the sort of judgments that can be true or false; and we think they are true.

Assuming that they are true, what makes these judgments true and their denial false? Again, the natural view about such empirical matters is that there is some fact about the relative trajectory of the Earth and the sun, or about the weather on a particular day in a particular place, and these facts make it true that the Earth rotates around the sun, or that it was sunny in Edinburgh on 13 May 2013.

Moreover, importantly, these facts seem to be independent of who I am or what cultural group I belong to. Of course, it's a fact about me that I know these facts. And it's a fact about my culture that (1) is a widely accepted part of our cosmological theory and (2) would be accepted by anyone who witnessed the weather in Edinburgh on that particular day. But that doesn't mean that these statements don't express objective facts about the relative trajectory of the Earth and sun and the weather in Edinburgh. If I were someone else or belonged to another culture, I might not believe that the Earth rotates around the sun, but the Earth would still rotate around the sun regardless of what I believe. If I didn't have the concept of a sunny day, I might not believe that it was sunny in Edinburgh on 13 May 2013, but it would still have been sunny in that particular place on that particular day.

We should recognize that issues get much more complicated when we consider the status of more fully worked out grand scientific theories, such Newtonian physics or Darwinian evolutionary theory. But if we focus just on specific empirical judgments, like the ones on the list above, a natural view is that these judgments are objectively true or false.

The reason I've been talking about the natural view about science is so that we have a template for understanding the objectivist view about morality, and we can understand the other views as rejections of the objectivist's answer to particular questions (A)–(C). The moral objectivist thinks our moral judgments, like the ones we listed above, are objectively true or false. From my examples, it's cases like the following that incline us to say 'yes, these statements are objectively true':

(5) The actions of Pol Pot were morally abhorrent.
(6) It's good to take care of your children.

If someone disagrees with (5) and says, for example, that the massive killing of people during the Khmer Rouge rule of Cambodia was not morally abhorrent, we're inclined to think they must just be mistaken. Perhaps there is some psychological or sociological explanation of how they came to have this crazy opinion, but I don't think there can be reasonable debate about the issue of whether genocide is morally abhorrent. Or if someone disagrees with (6) and says, for example, that taking care of your children isn't a very good thing to do – after all what did they ever do for you?! – we're inclined to think they've got the wrong end of the stick when it comes to being a good person. Again, there may be some explanation of how they came to have this strange view, but it's hard to imagine reasonable debate about the issue.

Perhaps that's incorrect, of course. It's examples like the following that put pressure on objectivism:

(3) Polygamy is morally dubious.
(4) Oedipus' sleeping with Jocasta was morally bad.

Many apparently reasonable people disagree, for example, about the morality of one man having multiple wives (or vice versa). Some say that it's OK in certain contexts; and it's obviously a practice that some people engage in. What do you think, is polygamy morally dubious? Also, some of you may feel that what Oedipus did wasn't morally bad, whatever the consequences, because he didn't know that Jocasta was his mother. What do you think, is incest always wrong, even if it is unknowing incest? According to objectivism, there is an objective fact of the matter, and when we disagree one side of the debate is right and the other wrong. And this is decided by the objective facts or so the objectivist says.

Before we discuss objectivism further, let's get two other philosophical theories about the status of morality on the table. The second theory I want to discuss is moral relativism.

Relativism

There are many forms of relativism, but the basic idea is that our moral judgments – expressed in statements like (3)–(6) – are indeed the sorts of things that can be true or false. So the relativist agrees with the objectivist about the answer to question (A). Unlike the objectivist, however, the relativist argues that moral judgments are true or false only relative to something that can vary between people. In this way, my judgment that polygamy is morally dubious might be true for me but false for someone else.

How is that possible? Well, it depends on the relativist's answer to question (B). One extreme form of relativism is **subjectivism**. This is the view that our moral opinions are relativized to each of our own subjective attitudes. For example, the subjectivist says that my statement 'Polygamy is morally dubious' is true just in case I morally disapprove of polygamy, but someone else's statement 'Polygamy is not morally dubious' is true just in case they do not morally disapprove of polygamy. Here's a rough analogy: it's like when I say 'Okra is yummy' and you say 'Okra is gross' – we might think that my assertion is true for me, even while your assertion is true for you. Both these statements might be thought to be made true by subjective facts about the individuals who assert them.

If our moral judgments are like this, it would explain why our moral opinions can seem very personal and why they are intimately tied up with motivation to action. However, this extreme form of relativism has a really hard time explaining the possibility of genuine moral disagreement. Unlike the example about okra, when it comes to polygamy, those who disagree are not usually prepared to chalk up their disagreement to a mere difference in taste. This motivates some philosophers to endorse a less extreme form of moral relativism. They claim that the truth of moral opinions is relative to culture. This view is sometimes called **cultural relativism**.

To get the basic idea, consider another rough analogy. When someone in Britain says 'One must always drive on the left' and someone in the US says 'One must never drive on the left', it's weird to ask: who is right? They're both right, for they are plausibly interpreted as making completely consistent claims that are simply relativized to different driving rules. That is, the statement made in Britain is true relative to the driving rules in Britain, while the statement made in the US is true relative to the driving rules in the US. Since these are non-overlapping jurisdictions, there's no real dispute. Of course, if the jurisdictions did overlap, there might be more than dispute – there might be traffic accidents!

The cultural-relativist view about the status of morality is similar. The relativist says that my judgment that polygamy is morally dubious could be true relative to my culture but someone else's judgment that polygamy is not morally dubious could be true relative to their culture. If that were the case, then there would be no real conflict. But what about the possibility of moral disagreement? Here the cultural relativist can argue that sometimes, even often, people find themselves in over-lapping cultures. And in these cases there is a real issue to dispute, something that matters: which actions are morally right or wrong relative to the culture shared by both people. But other times, where the cultures do not overlap, there is no real dispute.

Before evaluating this theory further, I want to introduce you to one more, final, general approach: emotivism.

Emotivism

Unlike all of the other philosophical views I've been discussing in this chapter, emotivism says that moral judgments aren't the sort of thing that can be true or false. According to emotivism, moral claims are neither statements of objective fact nor ones whose truth is subjective or culturally relative. They're expressions of our emotional reactions. So, the emotivist answers question (A) in the opposite way to the objectivist and the relativist. (As a result, questions (B) and (C) don't apply to emotivism.)

To get an idea of what emotivism comes to, recall the subjectivist view I discussed before. The subjectivist says that my statement 'Poly-gamy is morally dubious' is true just in case I morally disapprove of polygamy. The emotivist denies this, but she says instead that my assertion directly expresses my moral disapproval. In somewhat col-ourful language, the emotivist is suggesting that when I utter (3), it's as if I said 'Boo for polygamy!' thereby directly expressing my moral disapproval.

Although emotivists give a negative answer to question (A), they don't deny that we sometimes call some moral judgments true and others false in a loose sense. It's just that they think that, strictly speaking, our moral statements are not the expression of beliefs in matters of fact – neither objective nor relative facts – but rather the expression of our moral attitudes.

To explain the possibility of genuine moral disagreement, emotivists suggest that just as it's possible to disagree in belief, it's also possible to disagree in attitudes. Indeed, when I say 'Okra is yummy' and someone else says 'No, it's gross', it's plausible to construe what's going on as our both expressing attitudes towards okra – attitudes that disagree. That is, we might think I am expressing my like of okra and you are expressing your dislike. For the emotivist, moral disagreement is similar; it's disagreement in our moral attitudes, rather than in our beliefs about some matter of fact.

Objections and further directions

Let's take stock. So far in this chapter, I have introduced you to three philosophical approaches to questions about the status of morality – that is, theoretical answers to questions (A)–(C) about the status of moral judgments, like the ones we listed examples of above. Objectivism says that our moral judgments are definitely in the realm of truth and falsity – they're attempts at getting the objective facts about morality right. Relativism says that our moral judgments are in the realm of truth and falsity, but their truth and falsity is covertly relative to something like our subjective moral attitudes or our cultural norms. Emotivism says that our moral judgments are not really beliefs in matters of fact at all but rather the moral attitudes themselves. The statements which express them are not statements of fact but expressions of emotion.

Which of these views is the correct view to take about the status of morality? That's a big question that we're not going to resolve here. Indeed, in contemporary philosophical research, this is the foundational question of the subdicipline called **metaethics**. In metaethics, one can find a wide variety of views about the status of morality. And these views share some characteristics with one or more of the three approaches have outlined here, but the state-of-the-art metaethical theories are also more nuanced and refined. So, reaching a fully defensible view about the status of morality is an exciting but huge project.

Even if we can't resolve the issue here, we can get started thinking about this project by considering one main objection to each of the traditional theories. This will help you to understand the theories better. Plus, it is good philosophical methodology to refine our initial views in light of objections. So, a good research project would be to think about how we might refine each theory to get around the objection that I'm going to mention.

Let's start with an objection to the first theory we discussed: objectivism. At the beginning of this chapter we contrasted intuitions about empirical judgments and intuitions about moral judgments. In science, for example, we think we have a method that aims at the truth and which can resolve disputes with empirically gathered data. And although it is not as regimented, our everyday claims about the world around us – things like the weather or my height – also seem to be resolvable by observation. The same doesn't seem to be true of morality. Moral disputes, when we have them, often seem to be recalcitrant and unresolvable; there doesn't seem to be something like empirical data that could prove one side wrong and the other right. This seems like an important difference between morality and science which objectivism has a hard time explaining. That's the objection to objectivism: it can't explain this intuitive difference in our practices for resolving disputes about empirical judgments and for resolving disputes about moral judgments.

You might think that relativism makes better sense of this phenomenon. For it can say that we just need to investigate the moral norms of particular cultures to determine which moral judgments are true or false – of course, that's true or false relative to the particular culture in which they occur. However, there's an objection lurking for this theory too. If morality is relative to cultures, then it is difficult to make sense of moral progress. For example, many cultures in the past condoned slavery, but we've come to think that slavery is morally abhorrent. If relativism is right, that shift in opinion does not represent progress from a pervasive false opinion to a pervasive true opinion. For the relativist thinks that each moral opinion is made true or false relative to the culture in which it is made. The idea of intellectual progress seems like an important commonality between morality and science which relativism has a hard time explaining. That's the objection to relativism: it can't explain the possibility of moral progress.

Finally, what about emotivism? Well, if you follow the emotivist in thinking that moral statements are expressions of emotional reactions rather than beliefs in facts, then it becomes hard to explain the possibility of reasoning our way to our moral opinions. The emotivist might say that this is exactly the point of emotivism: our moral opinions aren't reasoned, they're emotional. However, even if it's true that emotions influence many of our moral opinions, it still seems that we can reason our way to some of our moral opinions. Indeed there is a well-known phenomenon of cognitive dissonance, where – as we say – one's head believes one thing even while one's heart feels something different. This shouldn't be possible if – as the emotivist suggests – moral opinions are really just feelings and not beliefs.

Is it possible to reply to these objections? Of course!

In response to the objection I mentioned for their view, objectivists could respond in at least one of two ways. First, they might argue that many moral disputes are resolvable by observing the world around us. For one of the things that seems to make actions right or wrong is their consequences – do they lead to good outcomes or bad outcomes? And this is something we might come to know by empirical investigation. However, even if the most important and fundamental moral questions aren't answerable by empirical investigation, objectivists have another avenue of response. They can argue that, even when there is no empirical method for resolving deep moral disputes, there can still be an objective one. Compare, for instance, the situation in mathematics. Mathematical disputes may be more arcane and theoretical, but they do occur among mathematicians. However, these disputes are not usually resolvable by collecting more observations about the world around us. Nonetheless, many mathematicians would regard them as disputes about some objective matter of fact. Similarly, you might think that the very issue that we've been discussing in this chapter – the status of morality – is not one that we can resolve by gathering empirical data but is none-theless one for which there must be some objectively correct answer. So, if you're inclined to favour objectivism, you might think about how there could be objective procedures for resolving moral disputes that are nonetheless interestingly different from the empirical methods of science. The procedures used in mathematical and philosophical research might provide good starting points.

In response to the objection I mentioned for relativism, defenders of this approach could respond by arguing that as long as we see previous generations as part of the cultural heritage of the present generation of some culture, then the moral statements of previous generations are to be evaluated according to the shared cultural norms. For example, if the founders of the United States are thought to overlap in culture with the contemporary generations in the US, then the statement 'Slavery is morally abhorrent' can be said to be true or false relative to this over-lapping culture. In this case, we think it is true. But that does raise an important question for the relativist: how do we tell which changes in opinion among a particular group represent improving views and which changes represent a new culture? Relatedly, what does it take for two cultures to 'overlap'? If you tend to think some form of moral relativism is right, you should think about how to answer these sorts of questions in a fully convincing fashion.

Finally, in response to the objection above to their view, emotivists often argue that we need to recognize the possibility of the reason-ableness or unreasonableness of evaluative attitudes just as much as beliefs in facts. For instance, it's natural to think that preferring (i) chocolate to beer, (ii) beer to sex, but (iii) sex to chocolate, is inconsistent and therefore unreasonable. If that's right, however, then it seems like there can be reasons for and against particular preferences, even though preferences aren't beliefs in facts. Indeed, some who are attracted to emotivism have argued that there's something not quite right about the idea that moral attitudes are emotive reactions, since this suggests that they are outside the realm of reason. A refinement of emotivism is sometimes called expressivism, which says that moral statements express moral attitudes, which are not factual beliefs, but which respond to reasons somewhat like preferences do. So, if you were initially attracted to emotivism, you might think about taking preferences as your model and trying to develop an account of the sorts of distinctively moral attitudes you think are expressed by moral statements.

Is it possible to object to these responses to the objections? Of course! That may seem exasperating, but if you can see how pursuing these lines of philosophical debate can help you weigh the theoretical costs and benefits of various theses in order to improve your own view about morality, you will have also started to appreciate the fun in serious philosophical debate.

Chapter summary

- One of the branches of the philosophical study of ethics is metaethics. The foundational question of metaethics is about the status of morality.
- The status of morality can be investigated by considering the answer to three questions listed above.
- Three basic approaches are objectivism, relativism, and emotivism.
- Objectivism says that our moral judgments are definitely in the realm of truth and falsity – they're attempts at getting the objective facts about morality right. This view purports to make sense of our intuitions about statements like 'The actions of Pol Pot were morally abhorrent', but it faces the objection that it cannot explain the intuitive difference between disputes about empirical facts and about moral issues.
- Relativism says that our moral judgments are in the realm of truth and falsity, but their truth and falsity is covertly relative to something like our subjective moral attitudes or our cultural norms. This view purports to make sense of our intuitions about morally relevant practices that seem to differ between very different cultures or people – e.g. polygamy. However, it faces the objection that it cannot make sense of moral progress.

- Emotivism says that our moral judgments are not really beliefs in matters of fact at all but rather the moral attitudes themselves. The statements which express them are not statements of fact but expressions of emotive attitudes. This view makes sense of the way our moral views seem to be evaluative and so capable of motivating action in a distinctive way. For that, however, it faces the objection that it cannot make sense of the possibility of reasoning rationally about some moral question.
- In contemporary metaethics, there are a large number of competing theories that share features with one of more of these three basic approaches. Deciding which one is correct is a matter of weighing theoretical costs and benefits by considering the advantages of each theory, as well as the objections and replies.

Study questions

1 Come up with new examples of an empirical judgment and a moral judgment. Explain in your own words what makes the former empirical and the latter moral.

2 Consider the statement 'Kicking dogs for fun is not wrong.' Which of the three main approaches to the status of morality discussed in this chapter hold that this statement can be true or false?

3 Why does relativism seem to be the right view to take about the statement 'One must drive on the left hand side of the road'?

4 What is subjectivism a form of? Explain your answer.

5 It seems to be possible to make moral progress. Give an example of this not discussed in the chapter and explain why this example causes problems for relativism.

6 Which of the following claims are inconsistent with moral objectivism? (a) Human reason cannot understand the ultimate truths about morality. (b) Most people's morals are corrupted. (c) Moral 'truth' is only a matter of opinion. (d) If a moral code is not supported by scientific evidence, then that moral code is false.

7 Emotivists claim that moral statements aren't, strictly speaking, true or false. What's another kind of statement that you might argue is not, strictly speaking, true or false? Explain your answer.

Introductory further reading

Blackburn, S. (2002) *Being Good: A Short Introduction to Ethics,* Oxford: Oxford University Press. (A very accessible introduction to some of the main themes in ethics, including metaethics.)

Chrisman, M. (2013) 'Emotivism,' in H. Lafollette (ed.) *International Encyclopedia of Ethics,* Chichester: Wiley-Blackwell. (A fuller introduction to emotivism, including its historical roots.)

Harman, G. and Thomson, J. J. (1996) *Moral Relativism and Moral Objectivity,* Malden, MA: Blackwell. (An accessible debate between a prominent proponent of relativism and a prominent proponent of objectivism.)

Schroeder, M. (2010) *Noncognitivism in Ethics,* New York: Routledge. (A book length introduction to non-cognitivist theories such as emotivism.)

Shafer-Landau, R. (2004) *Whatever Happened to Good and Evil?*, New York: Oxford University Press. (A very accessible introduction to some of the main themes in ethics, including metaethics.)

Advanced further reading

Chrisman, M. (2011) 'Ethical Expressivism,' in C. Miller (ed.) *The Continuum Companion to Ethics,* London: Continuum. (An introduction to the expressivist heirs to the emotivist tradition, including discussion of very contemporary versions of the expressivist theory.)

Mackie, J. L. (1977) *Ethics: Inventing Right and Wrong,* London: Penguin. (Influential defence of the idea that there are no moral facts.)

Miller, A. (2013) *An Introduction to Contemporary Metaethics,* 2nd edn, Cambridge: Polity. (Widely used textbook for university-level metaethics courses.)

Prinz, J. J. (2007) *The Emotional Construction of Morals,* New York: Oxford University Press. (Argument that morality is based on emotional responses and that these responses are inculcated by culture.)

Smith, M. (1994) *The Moral Problem,* Oxford: Blackwell. (Influential defence of a form of objectivism in metaethics.)

Williams, B. A. O. (1985) *Ethics and the Limits of Philosophy,* Cambridge, MA: Harvard University Press. (A very influential book attacking the objectivity of morality.)

Internet resources

Gowans, C. (2008) 'Moral Relativism', in E. Zalta (ed.) *Stanford Encyclopedia of Philosophy* [online encyclopedia] (Spring 2012 edn), http://plato.stanford.edu/entries/moral-relativism/. (A sophisticated introduction to relativism.)

LaFollette, H. (ed.) (2013) *International Encyclopedia of Ethics* [online encyclopedia], Wiley-Blackwell, http://onlinelibrary.wiley.com/book/10.1002/9781444367072. (Very comprehensive encyclopedia of articles by top researchers in the field introducing topics in ethics.)

A Bibliography of Metaethics, compiled by James Lenman, University of Sheffield [website], www.lenmanethicsbibliography.group.shef.ac.uk/Bib.htm. (Very comprehensive bibliography of papers published in metaethics.)

Interviews with Geoff-Sayre McCord (on metaethics), by Will Wilkinson, *Bloggingheads.tv* [blog], 6 June, http://bloggingheads.tv/videos/1562.

Sayre-McCord, G. (2012) 'Metaethics', in E. Zalta (ed.) *Stanford Encyclopedia of Philosophy* [online encyclopedia], http://plato.stanford.edu/ entries/metaethics/. (A sophisticated overview of contemporary issues in metaethics.)

5 Should you believe what you hear?

Matthew Chrisman,
Duncan Pritchard and
Alasdair Richmond

Introduction

In this chapter we will discuss a further issue in epistemology (a topic we previously covered in Chapter 2), but in doing so we will also introduce an important debate in the history of modern philosophy. This epistemological issue is the extent to which we should form our own beliefs based on the **testimony** of others. By testimony, philosophers typically mean more than just the sort of evidence one might give in a court of law or to a police investigation. They mean anything one hears or reads about from other people rather than witnessing or deducing it oneself. (So, for example, what you are reading right now counts as testimony from the authors of this chapter.)

Much of what we believe rests on testimony in this sense. Think, right now, of the many things that you believe, such as your belief about what the capital of Venezuela is, or your belief about how a television works. You will undoubtedly find that many of these beliefs were acquired by listening to the word of others, either directly (e.g. by being told these 'facts' by someone, such as a teacher), or indirectly (e.g. by reading these 'facts' in a textbook, or hearing them being said in a documentary). Moreover, notice that a great deal of what you believe on the basis of testimony could only be acquired in this way. There are many things that one simply couldn't reasonably find out for oneself, and where we need to trust the word of others if we are to form a judgment at all. Clearly, however, one shouldn't believe *just anything* that one is told; that is a recipe for gullibility. So how does one decide when to form one's beliefs on the basis of testimony, and when not to?

This particular epistemological question was a central issue in **the Enlightenment**, which was an important period of intellectual history, roughly from 1700 to 1800. It was during this period that ideas like reason, science and democracy were on the rise, while ideas like divine rule, religious revelation and tradition were under pressure. Scotland was an important area where the Enlightenment got a foothold, and Scottish intellectuals played a key role in this vibrant period of intellectual change.

A key figure of the Scottish Enlightenment was David Hume (1711–76). While he is now mostly known as a philosopher, in his lifetime he was almost certainly more widely known as an historian (his *History of England* was a best-seller of its day). His masterpiece *A Treatise of Human Nature* (1739) is still widely regarded as one of the best pieces of philosophical writing ever. It is famous for its rigorous empiricism, naturalistic world view and sceptical conclusions. Hume's empiricist idea was that everything that can be known will be known when it is known through careful empirical observation. This led him to seek naturalistic explanations of various phenomena about the human mind and will. This means that, unlike many of his contemporaries, he was sceptical of supernatural explanations. So rather than appealing to the power of God or the spirit inside of us to explain observable phenomena in the human mind, he sought to apply the same empirical scientific method that was at the time becoming more and more entrenched in the explanation of other natural phenomena. Because of this, Hume was very sceptical of religion.

This connects to the topic of this chapter because Hume was sceptical of miracles, especially of the sort that we read about in religious texts such as the Bible. The connection to the topic of this chapter is that most people learn about miracles not by witnessing them first hand but rather by hearing or reading about them from other people – that is, through testimony. In section 10 of his *Enquiry Concerning Human Understanding* (1748), Hume argued that we almost certainly won't find compelling testimony to miracles. We will discuss his argument in more detail below.

In his own day, the main opponent of Hume's view about miracles and testimony was **Thomas Reid** (1710–96). He was a minister in the Church of Scotland and a Professor at the Universities of Aberdeen and Glasgow. He was most famous for his defence of common sense. In his most influential work, *An Inquiry into the Human Mind on the Principles of Common Sense* (1764), he wrote,

> If there are certain principles, as I think there are, which the constitution of our nature leads us to believe, and which we are under a necessity to take for granted in the common concerns of life, without being able to give a reason for them – these are what we

call the principles of common sense; and what is manifestly contrary to them, is what we call absurd.

(1764/1997: ch. 2, §6, 33)

This is an expression of his idea that we are innately endowed with a propensity to think and feel certain things, and that we should trust in this endowment: to do so is to trust in common sense.

As we will see, the debate between Hume and Reid about testimony comes down to whether there must be independent reasons to trust the testimony of others or whether that's already an element of common sense. But before we get there, it will be useful to note how this ties in with the views of another famous Enlightenment figure, **Immanuel Kant** (1724–1804). Kant was a German philosopher who wrote several of the most influential works in philosophy. In his philosophy of mind, he stressed the interplay between the passive receptivity of the senses and the active application of concepts in human experience. In his ethical theory, he stressed the importance of **autonomy**, which is the sort of freedom one has when one is self-determining; i.e. where one determines one's own destiny, rather than having it determined by others. In a famous essay, 'An Answer to the Question: "What Is Enlightenment?"' (1784), he argued that 'enlightenment' is humanity's progressing from the immaturity of blindly following traditional dogma to the critical use of our own reason. In this promotion of what is now called 'intellectual autonomy', Kant's practical philosophy and theoretical philosophy merge. We are free in Kant's view when we think for ourselves. Later in this chapter we will discuss how the debate about testimony connects with Kant's view.

Our plan for the rest of the chapter is to introduce Hume's view on miracles and testimony. Then we will consider Reid's response to Hume. Next we will discuss the influence Hume had on Kant with respect to this particular issue. Finally, we will conclude by briefly exploring the connections between this issue in the history of modern philosophy and contemporary debates in epistemology about testimony.

Hume on miracles and testimony

A very important philosophical view about testimony finds a clear (and enduringly controversial) defence in the work of Hume. Hume advanced a view of testimony which suggested that there are certain kinds of events which are very difficult to make credible on the basis of testimony alone. In particular, Hume argued that testimony to any miraculous occurrence was almost certainly not going to be compelling.

Hume held that much of what we take for granted cannot be *rationally* justified but is justified by instinct and habit. Famously, Hume did not believe that our expectations that the future will resemble the past (or that the unobserved must resemble the observed) could be justified in a way that was both rational and non-circular. This is the famous problem of induction: how do we justify projections from what we have observed to what we haven't observed? Even our best-supported inductions can let us down. Hume considered two ways in which our inductions could be justified – either by logic or by experience. Neither, he concluded, offered a non-circular justification of induction.

Firstly, inductions do not express any 'relation of ideas' (or **conceptual truth**). The contradiction of a relation of ideas is inconceivable (or nonsensical), whereas the contrary of any induction, no matter how well-supported, is always conceivable: '*That the sun will not rise tomorrow* is no less intelligible a proposition, and implies no more contradiction, than the affirmation, *that it will rise*' (1748/1975: §4, pt I). However, neither can induction be justified as a 'matter of fact' or **empirical truth**. All inferences from experience must presuppose the principle of induction, hence that principle is too fundamental to be justified by appeal to experience: 'For all inferences from experience suppose, as their foundation, that the future will resemble the past' (1748/1975: §4, pt II). Likewise, attempts to justify induction by reference to the uniformity of nature face the insuperable obstacle that any belief in such uniformity can itself only be justified by induction. So the principle of induction is not susceptible to non-circular justification by reason or experience. However, Hume said we can explain our inductive habits, our tendency to project from experience, by reference to *instinct*: just as chickens are born with an instinct to scratch which serves them well in the farmyard, so human beings are born with an instinct to generalize from experience – and this instinct in turns serves us well in the wider world (pretty much). However, just as scratching is not a guarantee of immortality for chickens so induction can (and often does) lead us astray.

Hume's view of what counts as correct reasoning is roughly thus: reasoning correctly is not so much a matter of which beliefs you have, but more a matter of how you *change* your beliefs in the face of new evidence. Rational beings proportion their degree of belief to their best available evidence:

A wise man, therefore, proportions his belief to the evidence. In such conclusions as are founded on an infallible experience, he expects the event with the last degree of assurance, and regards his past experience as a full *proof* of the future existence of that event.

(1748/1975: §10, pt I)

Importantly for our purposes, Hume believed that testimony ordinarily carries with it important evidential weight but that it is not infallible. We must also take into account the probability of the event being testified to when assessing the weight of testimony. Hume's view of testimony has important links with his views on religion and his wider philosophy generally. In 'Of Miracles', the controversial tenth chapter of his *Enquiry Concerning Human Understanding*, Hume considers whether we could ever be rationally justified in accepting that a miracle has occurred based on someone else testifying that such a miracle had occurred.

Hume grants that, ordinarily, evidence derived from testimony has a powerful evidential force and would normally be decisive – i.e. normally testimony amounts to a practically sufficient proof of what is testified to. We are so built that we tend to favour the evidence of testimony, unless we have good reason to doubt that testimony. Ordinarily, we give testimony compelling evidential weight – human life would quickly become impossible if we couldn't take some claims on trust and we had to verify every single claim for ourselves.

However, our expectation that a law of nature will continue is also a proof (in Hume's sense of the term). Hume says uniform experience of any sequence of events should beget a powerful expectation it will continue, so any interruption of a law of nature will ordinarily be unbelievable, barring very strong evidence to the contrary. Such unbroken uniformities should have (at least psychologically) overwhelming evidential weight. Hume thought a law of nature was a projection of one of the best-confirmed regular sequences of events we possess. So we could speak of, for example, laws of nature that the sun will continue to rise everyday, that decapitation is quickly followed by death, or that air will continue to be breathable. So, while it is theoretically always possible that such hitherto unbroken uniformities could fail, we can have 100 per cent personal certainty they will continue. That is, interruptions may be possible but, prior to experience, they are *incredible* (not believable). Hume did not think that our belief in the continuation of laws of nature must be infallible – it is always possible that laws of nature may fail. But Hume thought that it is a psychological truth about human nature that uniform experience of an event sequence will beget powerful expectations that this sequence will continue.

By Hume's definition, a miracle is a violation of the laws of nature – i.e. an exception to one of the best-confirmed regularities we possess.

So this is why there is a problem about testimony of miracles for Hume: testimony to a miracle creates a tension between our instinct to believe testimony and our instinct to believe in the continuance of laws of nature. Which way should we then incline if testimony and laws of nature apparently conflict? If it seems more likely the testimony is distorted or mistaken, then we should reject the testimony and the miracle that the testimony is intended to support.

In particular, Hume argues that testimony diminishes in force if:

The event testified to is extraordinary,
We suspect partiality in the witnesses,
The testimony is not of good quality,
The event testified to is located long ago and/or far away, etc.

Given what we know about human nature, Hume says that we ought always to be suspicious of testimony in favour of the miraculous. People always tend to amplify stories of remarkable events, and can often deceive themselves (unconsciously or otherwise) in pursuit of their beliefs. Testimony to miracles is invariably at several removes from the eyewitnesses themselves, and the setting of the miracle is usually far away in space and time. Hume further concludes that no testimony could oblige us to believe a miracle had taken place in such a way as to support a religious hypothesis. However, Hume explicitly countenances at least the *possibility* of a rationally formed, testimony-based belief in the occurrence of a miracle and cautions his readers against reading too strong a conclusion into his argument:

> I beg the limitations here made may be remarked, when I say, that a miracle can never be proved, so as to be the foundation of a system of religion. For I own, that otherwise, there may possibly be miracles, or violations of the usual course of nature, of such a kind as to admit of proof from human testimony; though, perhaps, it will be impossible to find any such in all the records of history.
> (1748/1975: §10, pt II)

Hume's 'Of Miracles' is in two parts. Part I defines the problem: we instinctually trust testimony but we also instinctually expect laws of nature to continue. Both instincts are hard-wired in us for good reason. Life would be impossible if we weren't wired up thus. Normally, these instincts don't conflict, but they do conflict in the case of miracles. What to do? In Part II, Hume tries to resolve the tension: if you look at miracle testimony, you'll find that although a testimonially supported miracle is theoretically possible, in practice actual miracle testimony falls far short of the required standard. Hume says this: only if it would be more miraculous that the testimony was wrong than it would be for the testimony to be right can we accept testimony to a miracle. However, in practice, it will almost always be more rational to assume that testimony in favour of a miracle is flawed, either accidentally or deliberately, than to overturn all our best-confirmed theories and accept that the laws of nature have indeed been suspended. (Note Hume was concerned only with *testimony* to miracles – he never said for example that one would be obliged to reject the evidence of one's own senses if faced with the apparently miraculous.)

Some commentators have argued either that Hume ruled out miracles by definition or failed to allow that sufficient independent testimony might be compelling. Both claims are untrue. Hume clearly allowed that a miracle (or violation of the laws of nature) could occur and could even (theoretically at least) be the subject of compelling testimony. Consider Hume's 'eight days of darkness' example:

> Thus, suppose, all authors, in all languages, agree, that, from the first of January 1600, there was a total darkness over the whole earth for eight days: suppose that the tradition of this extraordinary event is still strong and lively among the people: that all travellers, who return from foreign countries, bring us accounts of the same tradition, without the least variation or contradiction: it is evident, that our present philosophers, instead of doubting the fact, ought to receive it as certain, and ought to search for the causes whence it might be derived. The decay, corruption, and dissolution of nature, is an event rendered probable by so many analogies, that any phenomenon, which seems to have a tendency towards that catastrophe, comes within the reach of human testimony, if that testimony be very extensive and uniform.
>
> (1748/1975: §10, pt II)

This kind of event could scarcely fail to be mentioned by every historian who treats of the period and to have had a cascade of effects thereafter. (For example, travellers from foreign lands everywhere record that the tradition of this darkness survives abroad.) The occurrence of such a uniquely public event, testified to universally by all who discuss the period, involving a violation of previously exceptionless and theoretically well-supported regularities, could in Hume's view be established by testimony. So, Hume doesn't rule out miracles by definition or that there could be enough evidence by testimony to believe in them.

The 'eight days of darkness' example shows Hume willing to stick his neck out and nominate (in detail) a case where belief in a miracle could be made compelling through testimony alone. The testimony has to be very strong and the event has to be of a very widely witnessed nature, but Hume's naturalistic philosophy did allow at least the *possibility* of a rationally formed, testimony-based belief in the occurrence of a miracle. However, Hume clearly thought no historical miracle had been supported by sufficiently good evidence to make belief in its occurrence compelling. Compare Hume on the 'eight days of darkness' case with his rejection of any reports of Elizabeth I's death and resurrection, even if these occurrences were universally endorsed by historians. In this latter case, the balance of proof would favour scepticism.

So Hume allows miracles can happen and can even be the subject of compelling testimony but he rejected the idea that miracle testimony could be made a compelling support for a particular religious hypothesis. Hume definitely does not say that miracles can never occur or that any occurrence must be non-miraculous by definition. Hume is concerned particularly with those miraculous events that are capable of acting as support for a system of religion, i.e. 'testimonial' miracles, miracles that testify to the divine mission, inspiration or guidance of a miracle worker. So what is at issue is whether miracle testimony could ever be good enough to make a miracle the foundation of a religious hypothesis. Hume did think that the task ahead of someone trying to make miracles compelling by testimony alone is a very steep task indeed and the task becomes worse (indeed impossibly worse) if the miracle concerned is supposed to offer uniquely compelling evidence for a given religious hypothesis.

Hume therefore clearly concludes that where an event testified to is sufficiently extraordinary (for example, if it involves the violation of a law of nature), the testimony has got to be of a very remarkable quality and quantity before it can become compelling. Hume also believed that when assessing the force of testimony, we should not attend merely to the reliability of the person (or persons) testifying; we should also consider the probability of the event whose occurrence the testimony is intended to support. Even very reliable witnesses might face a difficult task, even a practically almost impossible task, in making sufficiently unlikely events credible.

Reid's response to Hume

A very different account of how we should respond to testimony is offered by Reid. Reid argued that trusting testimony is akin to trusting one's senses. So just as when one sees that something is the case one does not always need an independent reason to trust one's senses (i.e. a reason for trusting one's sense which is not dependent on one's senses), the same applies in the case of testimony. If you see a table before you in normal circumstances, for example, then this can suffice to know that there is a table before you, without you having to determine an independent reason for trusting your senses in this regard (i.e. you don't need some general reason – not derived from one's senses – for trusting what one sees).

This is a very different conception of our reliance on testimony to that offered by Hume, who clearly felt that our reliance on testimony should often, if not always, be rooted in independent sources, such as our first-person observation of the informant's reliability. For Hume, while one can come to know that the object before one is a table just by seeing it, one cannot always comes to know something just by hearing it being testified to.

Reid also offered some considerations in support of his anti-Humean picture. In particular he appealed to what he took to be facts about our psychology to argue for two general principles about how we transmit and acquire our beliefs. According to the first, the so-called **principle of credulity**, we are naturally disposed to confide in others and believe what they tell us. According to the second, the so-called **principle of veracity**, we are naturally inclined to speak the truth and not to lie. With these principles in play, Reid argued that our psychology is such both that testimony is generally reliable (in line with the principle of veracity) and that we are in any case naturally inclined to trust testimony (in line with the principle of credulity).

Now one might think that Hume and Reid are arguing past one another here, in that Hume is talking about how we ought to form our beliefs on the basis of testimony, while Reid is merely describing how we in fact form our beliefs on the basis of testimony. So, for example, Hume can perfectly well accept that as a matter of fact we tend to trust the word of others (in line with the principle of credulity) and that we tend to speak the truth (in line with the principle of veracity), while at the same time contending that even so we ought not to trust the word of others and should seek an independent basis for trusting testimony (especially where that testimony concerns an incredible event, like the existence of a miracle).

A good way of illustrating this point is to consider what Reid says about how children acquire their beliefs. Here is Reid:

> if credulity were the effect of reasoning and experience [*as Hume claims*], it must grow up and gather strength, in the same

proportion as reason and experience do. But, if it is the gift of Nature, it will be strongest in children, and limited and restrained by experience; and the most superficial view of human life shews, that the last is really the case and not the first.

(1764/1997: ch. 6, §24, 195)

Reid's point is that if Hume's way of treating testimony were correct, then it would be a mystery how children acquire their beliefs. The child's path to knowledge, it seems, is via trust in their elders, and not by seeking an independent basis for trusting the testimony of others before accepting that testimony.

But we should be wary here. That children might well rightly trust the word of others is in principle consistent with what Hume outlines. In particular, Hume could argue that while children might well be practically obliged to trust their elders, what is important from an epistemological point of view is that normal mature adults are circumspect about the testimony they receive. Relatedly, while it might be true that we are generally disposed to tell the truth – a claim that is backed up by modern cognitive psychology by the way, which has developed ways of measuring the stress caused by lying – it could nonetheless be the case that testimonial deception is still extensive enough to warrant being sceptical about the evidence of testimony, at least the evidence of testimony other than one's own.

Intellectual autonomy: Hume and Kant versus Reid

This is a good juncture to introduce Kant into this debate. Kant was concerned to articulate the guiding principles which define enlightenment, and he did so in such a way as to effectively side with Hume in this debate. Here is Kant:

Enlightenment is man's emergence from his self-incurred immaturity. Immaturity is the inability to use one's own understanding without the guidance of another. ... The motto of the enlightenment is therefore: *Sapiere aude!* Have courage to use your own understanding.

(1784/1991: 54)

Kant thus regards a key element of enlightenment thinking that one should rely on one's own intellectual resources rather than trusting the word of another. In particular, Kant argued that the path to enlightenment required one to be sceptical about testimony in the sense that

Hume outlined, such that one always seeks an independent basis for trusting the word of another rather than taking that word at face value. For Kant, being sceptical about testimony is an essential part of intellectual autonomy, and thus of being autonomous more generally. That is, to be autonomous is to rationally determine one's own fate rather than having this dictated by others. To be specifically intellectually autonomous is to work out what one should believe by oneself rather than merely trusting the word of others, such as experts (e.g. religious authorities). To determine for oneself what one should believe inevitably requires that one should be sceptical about testimony, rather than taking it on trust. Kant thus sides with Hume against Reid on this issue, and regards the general scepticism about testimony that Hume advocates as being a key element of the enlightenment spirit of individual intellectual endeavour.

Note that Kant is not suggesting that the enlightened individual should have beliefs which are very different to those around her (though they might be), but only that they should intellectually 'own' those beliefs, even if they are commonplace. That is, intellectual autonomy does not require one to form one's beliefs in contrast to those around one (though it might in practice demand this), but it does mean that one cannot believe what one does *just because* others around one do so – instead, one must formulate the epistemic basis for believing in this way in a manner that is satisfactory from one's own intellectual perspective. Intellectual autonomy is thus a kind of epistemic 'owning' of the beliefs that one holds (i.e. as opposed to merely holding them because one has been taught them), just as autonomy more generally involves endorsing the basic values of one's life rather than simply accepting these values from others (which, note, is consistent with one endorsing the very same values as those around you – autonomy may lead one to having different values to those around you, but equally it might not).

The contemporary epistemological debate about testimony

The epistemological debate we have witnessed here as regards testimony lives on in contemporary philosophy. Very roughly, the debate now divides between two camps, known as **reductionism** and anti-reductionism (sometimes referred to as **credulism**).

The former camp takes its inspiration from Hume and argues for the importance of having an adequate non-testimonial basis for accepting testimonial claims. This is why the view is known as reductionism, in that in its strongest form it demands that one should always base one's beliefs acquired via testimony on non-testimonial evidence, and in this sense testimony is 'reduced' to non-testimonial sources. So, for example, on this view it's okay to accept someone's testimony if you have a track record of experience of the reliability of this person about the testified subject matter. In a sense, then, you are not basing your beliefs on your informant's testimony at all, but rather on your personal experience of their reliability.

The challenge facing reductionism is to explain why we don't end up lacking a lot of the testimonial knowledge we take ourselves to have. After all, as noted above, for a great deal of the beliefs which we acquired via testimony we lack any kind of non-testimonial basis for holding those beliefs (i.e. we only believe what we do because this is what we were told). So why then doesn't reductionism lead to a form of scepticism about testimonial knowledge?

The second camp takes its inspiration from Reid and emphasizes the importance of trusting others and their word as a route to knowledge. Credulists can easily evade the sceptical problem facing reductionism, since on this view testimonial knowledge is much easier to acquire. The problem this view faces is to explain why trusting others is not simply a recipe for gullibility. Put another way, if testimonial knowledge can be had even in the absence of non-testimonial evidence, then why should we think that it is a bona fide form of knowledge at all?

Chapter summary

- Testimonial knowledge is knowledge that we gain via the testimony of others. In the usual case, this will simply involve someone telling us what they know, but we can also gain testimonial knowledge in other more indirect ways, such as by reading the testimony of others (in a book like this one, say).
- A lot of what we believe depends on the testimony of others. Moreover, it is hard to see how we could verify for ourselves much of what we have been told via testimony, since such verification would itself involve making appeal to further testimony-based beliefs that we hold, and so would simply be circular.
- David Hume held that testimony is ordinarily a very powerful source of evidence and one that we instinctually favour. However, Hume also held that we have an instinct to expect laws of nature to continue unbroken. If a miracle is a violation of a law of nature, cases of testimony to miracles bring these two instincts into conflict. Hume argued that, in practice, it is overwhelmingly unlikely that testimony to a miracle will be of such good quality and come from

a sufficient number of disinterested witnesses to make it likely that the miracle occurred.

- In contrast to Hume, Reid argued that we should rely on testimony in the same way that we trust our senses – i.e. such that in both cases we can base belief on these sources without requiring an independent epistemic basis. To this end, Reid emphasizes relevant features of our psychology, in particular that we are naturally inclined both to tell the truth and to believe what we are told. But we saw that these considerations are moot in this context, in that Hume can consistently grant to Reid that we in fact form our testimonial beliefs in this way while nonetheless alleging that we ought not to do so.

- We saw that Kant effectively took sides with Hume in this debate by arguing that the spirit of the enlightenment was to seek one's own intellectual basis for holding one's beliefs (this is what we described as intellectual autonomy).

- We noted that the historical debate about testimony that we have examined here lives on in contemporary philosophy as part of the debate between *reductionism* and *credulism*. Reductionism claims that we need to be able to offer non-testimonial support for our testimony-based beliefs if they are to be rightly held. It faces the problem of explaining why this doesn't undermine much of the testimonial knowledge we take ourselves to have. Credulism in contrast argues that at least sometimes merely trusting the word of others can lead to testimonial knowledge. This view faces the problem of explaining why beliefs acquired in this way count as genuine knowledge.

Study questions

1 What is testimony, as philosophers think of it? Give some examples of beliefs that you hold which are based on testimony and some examples of beliefs you hold which are not based on testimony. In each case explain either why the basis for the belief in question is testimonial or non-testimonial.

2 Why can't we just believe everything we are told (i.e. all instances of testimony that are presented to us)? How might this lead us astray?

3 Why might it be problematic to refuse to form one's beliefs on the basis of testimony? How might this limit us?

4 Why does testimony to miracles create a tension in our beliefs, according to Hume?

5 How does Hume suggest that this tension can be resolved?

6 Did Hume believe that a miracle could be the subject of compelling testimony?
7 Did Hume believe that a miracle had ever been the subject of compelling testimony?
8 Is Hume correct in claiming that when assessing testimony, we need to take account not only of the reliability of the witnesses but also of the events being testified to?
9 In the discussion above of Hume and Reid a distinction is drawn between the way that we in fact form our testimonial beliefs and how we ought to form those beliefs. Check that you understand this distinction. Try to give an example to illustrate the distinction.
10 What does Kant mean when he says that intellectual autonomy is key to enlightenment?
11 Try to briefly state in your own words the reductionist and credulist views about the epistemology of testimony, and why someone might endorse these views. Which is preferable, do you think?

Introductory further reading

Lackey, J. (2011) 'Testimonial Knowledge', chapter 29 of S. Bernecker and D. H. Pritchard (eds) *The Routledge Companion to Epistemology*, London: Routledge. (A thorough and completely up-to-date overview of the main epistemological issues as regards testimony.)

Pritchard, D. (2013) *What Is This Thing Called Knowledge?*, 3rd edn, London: Routledge. (Chapter 8 offers a very accessible overview of the main issues with regard to the epistemology of testimony.)

Pritchard, D. and Richmond, A. (2012) 'Hume on Miracles', A. Bailey and D. O'Brien (eds) *The Continuum Companion to Hume*, London: Continuum, pp. 227–44. (A fairly accessible overview of some of the issues related to Hume's writings on miracles, and on testimony more generally, along with the relevance of these writings to the contemporary epistemological debate about testimony.)

Advanced further reading

Buchan, J. (2003) *Capital of the Mind: How Edinburgh Changed the World*, Edinburgh: Birlinn. (A useful account of Edinburgh's influence on the Enlightenment.)

Coady, C. A. J. (1992) *Testimony: A Philosophical Study*, Oxford: Clarendon Press. (This is the classic text on the epistemology of testimony which defends a credulist approach. Very readable (though perhaps not really introductory), with sections that apply the account of testimony offered to specific domains, such as legal testimony.)

88   *Chrisman, Pritchard and Richmond*

Coady, D. (2012) *What to Believe Now: Applying Epistemology to Contemporary Issues*, Chichester: Wiley-Blackwell. (A provocative contemporary treatment of the epistemology of testimony, which focuses on the relevance of the epistemology of testimony to issues in contemporary debate (e.g. the debate about climate change)).

Fogelin, R. J. (2003) *A Defense of Hume on Miracles*, Princeton, NJ: Princeton University Press. (Offers a thorough and sympathetic treatment of Hume on miracles.)

Hume, D. (1748/1975) *An Enquiry Concerning Human Understanding*, in *Enquiries Concerning Human Understanding and Concerning the Principles of Morals*, ed. L. A. Selby-Bigge, 3rd edn, Oxford: Oxford University Press. (Chapter 10 contains Hume's seminal argument regarding testimony and believing in miracles.)

Kant, I. (1784/1991) 'An Answer to the Question: "What Is Enlightenment?"', trans. H. B. Nisbet, in *Kant: Political Writings*, ed. H. Reiss, Cambridge: Cambridge University Press. (There are lots of good English translations of this text freely available on the web, such as this translation by Mary C. Smith hosted by Columbia University, www.columbia.edu/acis/ets/CCREAD/etscc/kant.html.)

Reid, T. (1764/1997) *An Enquiry into the Human Mind on the Principles of Common Sense*, ed. D. R. Brookes, Edinburgh: Edinburgh University Press. (Chapter 6, section 24 contains Reid's seminal argument for trusting testimony.)

Internet resources

Adler, J. (2012) 'Epistemological Problems of Testimony', in E. Zalta (ed.) *Stanford Encyclopedia of Philosophy* [online encyclopedia], http://plato.stanford.edu/entries/testimony-episprob/. (This is an outstanding and state-of-the-art entry on the epistemology of testimony, written by one of the experts in the field. It includes lots of detail about the debates in this area and a comprehensive list of references to other articles that might be of use.)

Green, C. (2008) 'Epistemology of Testimony', in B. Dowden and J. Fieser (eds) *Internet Encyclopedia of Philosophy* [online encyclopedia], www.iep.utm.edu/e/ep-testi.htm. (A comprehensive and very recent survey of the issues regarding the epistemology of testimony. Not for beginners.)

Morris, W. E. (2009) 'Hume', in E. Zalta (ed.) *Stanford Encyclopedia of Philosophy* [online encyclopedia], http://plato.stanford.edu/entries/hume/. (A helpful overview of the work of Hume.)

Yaffe, G. and Nichols, R. (2009) 'Reid', in E. Zalta (ed.) *Stanford Encyclopedia of Philosophy* [online encyclopedia], http://plato.stanford.edu/entries/reid/. (An excellent, and up-to-date, overview of the work of Reid.)

6   Are scientific theories true?

Michela Massimi

Introduction

This chapter introduces you to an area of philosophy called **philosophy of science**. Philosophy of science takes science as its main topic and focus. Science can provide the springboard for a variety of philosophical reflections, in at least two different ways.

(1) We can ask questions such as: what is science? What counts as scientific knowledge? How do our scientific theories track nature?

(2) We can ask more specific questions about specific branches of science (say, physics, chemistry, biology, medicine, psychology, economics, and so forth). For example, one may want to know what the nature of space-time is, according to our current best physical theories. Or, how we classify biological species and how we should think about them. Or, how effective randomized controlled trials are for testing new drugs in medicine, and so forth.

Philosophy of science, broadly understood, encompasses both kinds of questions, although the second kind of questions fall under the remit of specific branches of philosophy of science, such as philosophy of physics, philosophy of biology, philosophy of medicine, among others.

Philosophers of science aim to tackle important conceptual and foundational questions about science by engaging with both actual scientific practice, as well as with the history of science. Sometimes answering a question such as 'What is the nature of spacetime?' requires engaging with the details of relativity theory as much as with metaphysics, i.e. the branch of philosophy that deals with the question of what there is (e.g. should we think of space as a substance, for example?). Other times, answering a question such as 'How effective are randomized controlled trials for testing new drugs in medicine?'

requires knowing the details of the actual scientific practice no less than epistemology, i.e. the branch of philosophy that deals with general questions about knowledge.

But there are yet other times when an adequate answer to some of the conceptual and foundational questions about science requires not just knowing the details of current science, but also knowledge of the history of science. Often we can gain insights about conceptual questions by looking at how the relevant scientific field has evolved over centuries, what challenges it has faced, and how it has solved them. This distinctive way of tackling some of the relevant questions about science goes under the name of history and philosophy of science (or, briefly, HPS). Despite what the name might suggest, HPS is more than a mere conjunction of philosophy of science and history of science. Instead, HPS is a distinctive way of addressing philosophical questions about science by looking at the history of science, no less than at the current scientific practice.

In this chapter, I will follow an HPS approach to tackle the question: 'Are scientific theories true?'. This question falls under the first kind (1), above, as we won't be looking at specific scientific theories (say, relativity theory or quantum mechanics), or scientific fields (say, physics *versus* biology). Instead, we will be asking a general question about how science and our scientific theories track nature, so to speak. In tackling the question of whether our scientific theories are true, I will briefly discuss a famous episode in the history of science: the transition from Ptolemaic astronomy to Copernicanism and Galileo Galilei's defence of it. I will use this episode to illustrate two main philosophical views, known as **scientific realism** and **scientific antirealism**.

I'll introduce you to these two views and very briefly review the historical episode. Then, I'll discuss scientific realism: we will get clear about what the view amounts to, and explain the main argument in favour of scientific realism (the so-called no-miracles argument). We'll then take a closer look at the second view, scientific antirealism – or better, at a prominent variety of it called **constructive empiricism**. Finally, in the concluding section, we'll consider two famous realist objections to constructive empiricism.

Two grand traditions: a very short history

Imagine a starry night, with the sky so clear that you can almost count the number of the stars and observe with the naked eye some of the planets in our solar system. Now, imagine that you observe the sky for many nights in a row, over a period of months, and suppose you are meticulous enough to record on a piece of paper the relative positions of the visible celestial bodies with respect to the stars from your chosen vantage point. What you are likely to observe, if you follow a sort of join-the-dots game, is that the visible planets move over months with respect to what – to the naked eye – appear as 'fixed stars' in the background. But the motion of the planets that you are likely to observe is not along any straight line. Instead, the join-the-dots game would soon reveal that planets seem to move on a straight line up to a point, then curl up, form a little loop, and then continue to move along a straight line.

This phenomenon has a name: it is called retrograde motion of planets. What explains it? Well, it depends on which astronomical theory you consider; but it will also depend – in a more subtle way – on what we take to be the aim of astronomy (and science, more generally). So, what is the aim of science? There are two grand traditions that we should consider here.

According to the first tradition, the aim of science (in our example, the aim of astronomy) is to be accurate, to provide us with a good description and a good analysis of the available evidence in any particular field of inquiry. In a word, we want our scientific theory (in our example, our astronomical theory) to account for the available phenomena (including the anomalous trajectory of the planets we have just observed and meticulously recorded). Philosophers of science have coined an expression for the generic 'to account for the phenomena': they say that we want our scientific theories **to save the phenomena**. The expression comes from the ancient Greek and it literally means 'to save the appearances'. Thus, we may think of scientific theories, in astronomy for example, as providing us with hypotheses (namely, suppositions that have not yet been established either on theoretical or experimental grounds), and we may expect these hypotheses to fit or match the available appearances, without necessarily having to be true about those appearances, or to tell us a true story about how they came about, what their causes might be, or what the underlying physical mechanism for their production might look like. We will see in the next section that ancient Greek astronomers, for example, came up with the hypothesis of epicycles and deferents to save the phenomenon of the retrograde motion of the planets.

According to the second tradition, the aim of science is not just to save the phenomena, but rather to tell us the truth about the phenomena. But what is truth? By 'truth', philosophers of science mean that the scientific theory gets things right, or, that what the theory says about those phenomena (for example, what the theory says about the causes of the phenomena and their underlying physical mechanisms) *corresponds* to the way things really are in nature. We can think of truth as a relation of correspondence between what the scientific theory says about, for example, the retrograde motion of the planets, and what is really the case about it in nature. Often to tell a true story about a particular phenomenon (or range of phenomena in a given domain) requires hypothesizing the existence of some scientific objects (e.g. particles, forces) or other, that may prove elusive not only to the human eye, but also to detection via sophisticated technological devices. In our chosen example, to tell a true story about the retrograde motion of the planets as an illusory motion (due to the different relative velocities of the planets with respect to the Earth, our observational vantage point, which also moves around the sun), we would need to introduce gravitational force as the cause of orbital motion, and clarify the underlying physical mechanism for planetary motion.

There is an important distinction between the phenomena (for instance, the retrograde motion of planets) and the underlying scientific entities (for instance, gravitational force) that one may introduce to tell a true story about the phenomena and their underlying mechanism. The distinction does not quite run parallel to that between appearances and reality, but it comes close. For now, let us take phenomena to mean all the available evidence (I will introduce a further distinction about *observable* phenomena in discussing van Fraassen's constructive empiricism, pp. 97–101). And let us take scientific entities to refer to things such as gravitational force, neutrinos, electrons, bacteria, DNA strands, and so forth. The latter are introduced by scientific theories with the purpose of telling a true story about the phenomena. For example, the entity in question can act as the cause of the phenomena. Or, it can be involved in the mechanism that brings about the phenomena, or similar.

The first tradition that sees the aim of science as that of saving the phenomena goes under the name of scientific antirealism. The second tradition, which takes truth as the ultimate goal of science, is known as scientific realism. Both these traditions were defended and advocated in the course of the history of science. The first one, most notably, in ancient Greek astronomy; the second became the hallmark of Galileo's scientific revolution.

From Ptolemaic astronomy to Copernican astronomy

The dominant astronomical theory in ancient Greek times was Ptolemaic astronomy. Ptolemy was a Greek-Roman astronomer in the second century AD, whose astronomical treatise *Almagest* had huge influence for centuries to come. Building on Aristotle's physics, Ptolemaic astronomy regarded the cosmos as organized and structured in a series of orbital shells, along which all planets (including the sun, which at the time was regarded as a planet) orbit around the Earth. This was the simplest astronomical hypothesis for planetary motion: the Earth seemed still at the centre of the cosmos, with all the other celestial bodies rotating around it, in agreement with the available evidence and observations. Yet the hypothesis required some tweaks and fudges in order to explain anomalous phenomena, such as the retrograde motion of the planets. To 'save this phenomenon', Ptolemaic astronomy had to introduce a complex system of circles, whereby each planet moved along a circular orbit called an epicycle, whose focus was in turn rotating along a larger circular orbit called a deferent. By assuming that planets moved along epicycles and deferents, Ptolemaic astronomy was able to save the phenomenon of retrograde motion. Yet Ptolemaic astronomers were aware that their complex system of epicycles and deferents was just an astronomical hypothesis to save the phenomena.

The French philosopher Pierre Duhem in the early twentieth century wrote a short but illuminating book, entitled *To Save the Phenomena* (Duhem 1908/1969), where he offered his own interpretation of the history of physical theories from Plato to Galileo. Duhem claimed that for centuries, back to Ptolemy, the aim of astronomy was to provide hypotheses that could match the available evidence, without any claim of being true. Indeed, ancient astronomers knew well that there could have been more than one hypothesis compatible with the same evidence. Duhem called it 'the method of the astronomer'. Given this tradition, it is no wonder that when in 1543 Copernicus' book *De revolutionibus orbium coelestium* (*On the Revolutions of the Celestial Spheres*) was published, the revolutionary heliocentric hypothesis was very modestly presented as just another hypothesis (albeit a promising one) to save the phenomena.

Despite the understated tone of the dedicatory letter, Copernicus did not disguise his belief in the superiority of his astronomical theory over the fictitious hypotheses of his predecessors. But Copernicus died the same year his book was published, and an anonymous preface accompanied the book, carefully crafted by Andreas Osiander, who mitigated the spirit of Copernicus' work by presenting it as yet another exercise in the well-trodden astronomical tradition of saving the phenomena. No wonder the publication of Copernicus' book did not set religious authorities aflame, until almost a half-century later, when Galileo Galilei dared to overthrow the received view of astronomy as *saving the phenomena,* and to say that Copernican astronomy was true of the heavens.

In the summer of 1609, Galilei built his first telescope, following similar attempts in the Netherlands. His first rudimentary telescope was used as a naval instrument in Venice to spot boats coming to port. A few months later, an improved and more powerful telescope was pointed at the moon and revealed mountains and craters that Galileo beautifully described in *The Starry Messenger.* It was unequivocal evidence that celestial bodies were very similar in nature to the planet Earth, *pace* the Aristotelian–Ptolemaic tradition. But even more amazing discoveries were around the corner: in January 1610 Galileo observed what he thought were four stars wandering around the planet Jupiter (i.e. Jupiter's satellites), and in December of the same year he could observe phases in the planet Venus (similar to lunar phases), which were impossible according to the Ptolemaic system. It was the triumph of Copernicanism. Convinced by the new experimental evidence, Galileo embraced Copernicanism not just as a hypothesis that could save the appearances, but as a physical truth that he believed could also be reconciled with religious truths in the Bible. It was the beginning of Galileo's dispute with the church and the rest is now history.

But from a philosophical point of view, what matters for our purposes is that Galileo defended what Duhem aptly called the 'method of the physicist' against the 'method of the astronomer'. For Galileo, astronomy (as any scientific discipline) must track nature, and get things right, as opposed to devising mathematical hypotheses and contrivances that could merely save the appearances. Galileo can be regarded as ushering in the view that science should tell us a *true* story about nature, and reveal the truth about the phenomena in question via mathematical demonstrations and indubitable principles. Galileo's scientific methodology is not just the hallmark of the scientific revolution, which eventually brought the demise of Ptolemaic astronomy. For our philosophical purposes here, Galileo is historically at the crossroads of two rival philosophical traditions about the aim of science. He was the first one to depart from the tradition of *saving the phenomena* and to champion a new view of science as being in the business of telling us a *true* story about nature. Regardless of one's opinion about the aim of science (saving appearances vs truth), the scientific advancement made possible by Galileo's discoveries remains unquestionable on either side of this philosophical divide. Indeed, the divide is not about Galileo's discoveries or achievements, but instead it is about what we take to be the aims of science. In the next two sections, I review in turn each of these philosophical traditions.

Scientific realism and the no-miracles argument

Scientific realists claim that the aim of science is to give us theories (be it Copernican astronomy, Newtonian mechanics or any other theory in any other field of inquiry), which once *literally construed*, we *believe* to be *true*. We need to clarify this definition, as there are at least three main distinct aspects involved in it (Psillos 1999; Chakravartty 2011; Ladyman 2002: ch. 5).

First, what does 'literally construed' mean here? The intuition is that we must take scientific theories at face value. In other words, we must understand and construe the *language* of the theory *literally* as referring to objects and entities in the real world, no matter how unobservable or elusive to detection those entities might be. This is the *semantic aspect* implicit in the above definition of scientific realism. For example, if our scientific theory talks about gravitational force, and we are realist about the theory, we must take the term 'gravitational force' as referring to, or picking out, a real force in nature. If our theory postulates a particle called a neutrino, and we are scientific realists, we must take the term 'neutrino' as picking out a real particle. The *semantic aspect* ensures that the language of the scientific theory is interpreted as mapping onto real objects in nature, and theoretical terms refer to real entities (observable or unobservable as they may be).

The other important aspect in the definition above is captured by the expression 'we *believe* to be true'. Scientific realism enjoins us to believe that our best scientific theories are true. This is a claim about what we ought to believe about science; as such, it captures an important *epistemic aspect*. The intuition is that whenever we accept a scientific theory, we commit ourselves to believing it. More precisely, we commit ourselves to believing that the theory is true, and not false; true, and not just useful; true, and not just mathematically elegant, or simple, or convenient, etc. So, once more, what is *truth*?

Here we touch upon a third important aspect in the definition of scientific realism, a properly *metaphysical aspect*. I said above that a theory is true if, roughly speaking, it gets things right; if it corresponds to states of affairs in the world. But what does *that* mean? The meta-physical intuition here is that what the theory says about its specific object of inquiry is capable of being either true or false, and what makes it true or false is not something about us, about our language, or our minds, or our concepts, or our perceptions. Instead it is some-thing about the *world* itself, and the way the world is independently of us, and what we think about the world. Even if Copernicus had never existed and even if we had developed a completely different scientific history from the one we did, it would still be the case that planets orbit the sun. This is a fact about nature, which is independent of us, of our minds, our language, and our concepts. This is the *metaphysical* intuition behind scientific realism. Take again as an example Copernican astronomy. Being realist about Copernican astronomy means you endorse the following claims:

(1) There are factual matters about planets and planetary motion that are *mind-independent* (i.e. they do not depend in any way on us, our minds, our concepts etc.) – this is the *metaphysical aspect*;
(2) The language of our theory, and its theoretical terms (e.g. 'planets', 'planetary motion', and so on) pick out objects in nature – this is the *semantic aspect*;
(3) Whatever the theory says about those objects (e.g. 'Planets orbit the sun') is true, or approximately true – this is the *epistemic aspect*.

I have added the qualification 'approximately true' because it is important to avoid a common cause of confusion. Scientific realists are neither so dogmatic nor so naive as to claim that science never gets things wrong. Of course, there are mistakes in science. Copernican astronomy maintained that planets travelled along circular orbits, and Kepler proved that it's actually elliptical orbits, for example. Newtonian mechanics entertained the idea that gravitational force was acting at a distance between celestial bodies, while relativity theory explains gravitational force in terms of how the mass–energy tensor shapes and warps spacetime. Scientific realists would say that these are two examples of scientific progress, whereby a later theory in mature science has replaced an earlier theory, by modifying or amending some of the relevant details. Should we then say that Copernican astronomy, or Newtonian mechanics were false? Not so fast, the realist would say. Instead, it seems more appropriate to say that these earlier theories were *approximately* true, they got things in part right, in part wrong, until they were replaced by *better* theories, which are more likely to be true. Truth is the goal at the end of the inquiry; and science, as a whole, is marching towards it. This is what scientific realism is ultimately committed to.

The perceptive reader will complain at this point that I have only given a definition of scientific realism. But what is the argument for it? Why should one be a scientific realist? The most prominent philosophical defense of scientific realism is called the no-miracles argument. It was originally formulated by the philosopher Hilary Putnam (1978) and says that one ought to be realist about science, because scientific realism is the only philosophy that does not make the success of science a miracle. The starting point of the argument is the hard-to-deny observation that science has proved very *successful* over time. Suppose we all agree on that observation. The realist then invites us to come up with an *explanation* for the success of science: why is it that we have theories that talk about gravitational force, or neutrinos, or other unobservable entities, and get things right? How come we can make predictions on the basis of these theories, and our predictions turn out to be right most of the time? How could Copernicus successfully predict the phases of Venus, despite the overcast sky of Poland, if his theory were not true? You get the gist of the no-miracles argument.

The argument says that we must be realist about science, because if we were not – if planets did not orbit the sun, and if the term 'planet' did not capture any real object, and if what Copernicanism tells us about planetary motion were not approximately true – then it would be just a miracle that Copernicanism has proved so successful in predicting the phases of Venus that Galileo observed, among other phenomena. The same can be said for Newtonian mechanics and relativity theory: if the term 'gravitational force' did not refer to any real force in nature, if what Newtonian mechanics says about gravitational force were not approximately true, then it would be just a miracle or a lucky coincidence that we have a theory that speaks of gravitational attraction and successfully predicts a great range of phenomena. To sum up, scientific realism seems to be the most plausible view if we want to be able to explain and make sense of why we have such undeniably successful science. Scientific theories must be true on pain of miracles and lucky cosmic coincidences.

A variety of scientific antirealism: Bas van Fraassen's constructive empiricism

But is that so? Should we really believe scientific theories to be true, to explain the tremendous success of science? The antirealist is not going to be impressed by the above argument. Scientific antirealism comes in several varieties. There are indeed at least three main varieties of antirealism, corresponding to the three different aspects of scientific realism that one may wish to reject.

First, one might reject the *metaphysical aspect* of scientific realism, and deny that there are facts of the matter about planetary motions, gravitational force, neutrinos, or any other object, *independently of us*. Denying that there are mind-independent facts about nature is typical of two main kinds of antirealism (among others): **constructivism** and

conceptual relativism. Constructivists contend that the objects of scientific inquiry are human or social constructions to some extent, and as such they do not enjoy the metaphysical status that scientific realism seems to cheerfully ascribe to them. Constructivists take seriously the lessons that seem to be coming from science studies about the socio-political aspects of scientific research and how they shape and influence research outputs. Conceptual relativists, on the other hand, do not go as far as claiming that scientific objects are human constructions; but they share with constructivists the denial of the *metaphysical aspect* about a mind-independent world. They would insist that there is no ready-made world and that scientific phenomena depend, in some sense, on our concepts or conceptual apparatus, and change as soon as the latter changes, for example, after a scientific revolution.

Second, one might reject the *semantic aspect* in the definition of scientific realism. While less popular than the previous option, *semantic antirealism* finds its expression in two main views. The first may be called **logical empiricism** in claiming that the language of science can be clearly divided into a theoretical vocabulary and an observational vocabulary, where the former encompasses all theoretical terms that refer to unobservable entities (say, 'neutrino', 'gravitational force', and so on) and is ultimately reducible to the observational vocabulary. The second form of semantic antirealism, **instrumentalism**, is the view that we should not take scientific language at face value and it does not matter what objects the theoretical terms of our theory may be picking out (for example, we could use the theoretical term 'light', without committing ourselves to the view that the term picks out electromagnetic waves anymore than streams of photons).

There is yet a third variety of antirealism, which without questioning either the metaphysical or the semantic aspect of scientific realism, plays down nonetheless the *epistemic* aspect. The view is known as constructive empiricism and has been advocated over the past twenty-three years by the American philosopher of science Bas van Fraassen. It is to this view that I want to dedicate my attention in the rest of this section, as it has been arguably the most serious contender in the debate between realism and antirealism over the past few decades.

What is constructive empiricism then? Constructive empiricists agree with the scientific realist that we must take scientific theories at face value, and construe the language of science literally. They also agree with the scientific realist about the metaphysical aspect, namely that there are facts of the matter in the world and objects and entities that exist mind-independently. But constructive empiricists contend, by contrast with the realist, that theories need not be true to be good. Or better, they contend that accepting a scientific theory does not imply *believing* that the theory is *true*. Instead, accepting a theory implies only the *belief* that the theory is *empirically adequate*. Thus, for constructive empiricism, the aim of science is not truth (or approximate truth), but instead empirical adequacy. More precisely, 'science aims to give us theories which are empirically adequate; and acceptance of a theory involves as belief only that it is empirically adequate' (van Fraassen 1980: 12). Empirical adequacy is, in turn, defined in terms of how our scientific models fit or match the available evidence. Echoing (loosely) what Duhem called the 'method of the astronomer', contemporary constructive empiricists do not see science as being in the business of telling us a true story about nature. Instead, they claim that we can still do justice to science, scientific progress and success without having to introduce the extra assumption that theories are true. Why is truth an extra assumption? One may point out that there are many examples of past scientific theories that were believed to be true and proved to be false (from the caloric theory in the late eighteenth century, whereby thermal phenomena were explained in terms of a substance called 'caloric', to the ether theory in the nineteenth century, where the ether was assumed to be the medium for both optical and electromagnetic phenomena). A powerful antirealist objection says that as past theories proved false, there is no guarantee that our current best theories will not similarly prove false. The objection is known as pessimistic meta-induction. It was not originally formulated by constructive empiricists but can be used by them, as an argument for the truth of our scientific theories, as by any other antirealist, to challenge the alleged success of science. Hence, if there is an alternative way of making sense of scientific success, which does not resort to the risky belief that theories are true (given that they might in fact prove false), so much the better for science! Truth may not be needed after all to explain the success of science, *pace* the no-miracles argument. Or so the constructive empiricist argues. We need then to get clear about **empirical adequacy** as a viable alternative to truth.

Van Fraassen (1980: 12) defines a theory as empirically adequate if what the theory says about the observable things and events in the world is true; in other words, a theory is empirically adequate if it saves the phenomena. The reference to the old adage of 'saving the phenomena' is not happenstance. Like Duhem, van Fraassen too defends a form of *empiricism* in claiming that scientific knowledge should be confined to the level of appearances or observable phenomena, things we can see and experience with the naked eye, without any further commitment to unobservable entities. By contrast with Duhem, however, van Fraassen has a more articulated view of how science is supposed to save the phenomena or match the available evidence. As the adjective 'constructive' in the name constructive empiricism suggests, van Fraassen sees an important element of construction at work in scientific inquiry, especially in the way scientists build models that must be adequate to the phenomena.

Scientific theories can indeed be regarded as families of models, whereby higher-level theoretical models are constructed and devised to save phenomena that may appear at the lower level of data models. How to define data models, how to construct theoretical models, and to understand the particular way in which van Fraassen envisages the process of 'fitting' theoretical models to data models (where phenomena may appear) is a long and complex story, which would require going through the vast literature on scientific models that I do not have the space to cover (see Morgan and Morrison 1999; Frigg and Hartmann 2012). Suffice it here to say that van Fraassen is part of a bigger trend in contemporary philosophy of science that has stressed the central role of scientific models, and how models can be useful and explanatory without necessarily providing a perfectly true representation of the target system. Instead I want to briefly go back to the empiricist component in van Fraassen's view, and clarify the difference from scientific realism. How can scientific knowledge be confined to the level of appearances or observable phenomena, without any further commitment to unobservable entities? How can empirical adequacy be a serious competitor to truth in our conception of the aim of science?

Constructive empiricists urge us to clearly demarcate between the observable and the unobservable. A theory is empirically adequate if it is saves all the (past, present and future) observable phenomena (not just the actually observed ones). A phenomenon is observable if it can, in principle, be observed by us with the naked eye, or unaided vision. Consider, for example, the moons of Jupiter. True, Galileo needed a telescope to observe them. Yet, under van Fraassen's criterion of observability, the moons of Jupiter count as in principle observable because in principle it is possible for us to *see* them with unaided vision (say, astronauts can board a spaceship, and take a closer look at them). Consider now a neutrino, or an electron, a piece of DNA strand, a bacterium, or other similar entities. There is no way we could ever achieve an unaided vision of any of these entities, i.e. without using more or less powerful microscopes (unless we resort to some science-fiction scenarios and we imagine ourselves able to shrink to some Lilliputian size to have a close-up of any of these entities). Neutrinos, electrons, DNA strands, bacteria, and so on count as *unobservable*.

But, surely, the vast majority of scientific entities seem to go well beyond the remit of observable phenomena as van Fraassen intends them. How serious is empirical adequacy, so defined, as an alternative to the realist's quest for truth? Constructive empiricists have a powerful argument in their defence of empirical adequacy as the ultimate aim of science. Indeed, they claim they can make perfect sense of why we have the incredibly successful science that we do in terms of our theories being empirically adequate. Van Fraassen (1980: 39) has provided what he calls a 'Darwinian' reformulation of the no-miracles argument, whereby the success of current science is neither a miracle nor a lucky coincidence. Scientific theories are born into a life of fierce competition and only the successful ones survive, i.e. those that latch onto actual regularities in nature and save the phenomena! Natural selection applied to scientific theories means that theories that prove to have the wrong observable consequences fail and get discarded, while theories that save the observable phenomena succeed and prove survival adaptive. We have abandoned the caloric theory and the ether theory, not because they were necessarily false (i.e. there is no such thing as the ether or the caloric as an unobservable entity). But rather because they did not save the observable phenomena. For example, the ether theory was known for not squaring well with the experimental evidence coming from the Michelson–Morley experiment in 1887. The caloric theory was at odds with Joule's paddle-wheel experiments in the 1840s about the interchangeability of mechanical work and thermal energy. Empirical adequacy is all we need to explain the success of science. Truth is an unnecessary extra assumption, and a potentially risky one.

Two realist objections to van Fraassen

Should we then give up scientific realism and embrace constructive empiricism? A considerable literature (see Churchland and Hooker 1985; Monton 2007) has grown over the past 20 years or so that in various ways has attacked the observable/unobservable distinction as untenable, arbitrary or epistemically questionable. Van Fraassen's view has been the focus of a heated debate and has left a significant mark in the philosophy of science landscape. In this final section, I review very briefly two prominent realist rejoinders to the challenge posed by constructive empiricism.

First, a response to the Darwinian reformulation of the no-miracles argument (Lipton 2004: 193; and Kitcher 1993: 156). One may reply that the Darwinian take on the no-miracles argument leaves scientific realism unscathed. One thing is to explain why only successful theories survive. Another thing is to explain why a theory is successful in the first instance. Suppose you want to explain why Alice, but not Sarah, got accepted to study for an undergraduate degree in philosophy at the University of Edinburgh, and your explanation is that only applicants with three *A*s in their final year's exams get an offer at Edinburgh. Well, this might be a Darwinian explanation of why only some students get an offer from Edinburgh (namely, those with three *A*s in their final year's exams). But it still does not explain why Alice got the offer (while Sarah did not), if what we are looking for is ultimately an explanation of why Alice (but not Sarah) got three *A*s in the final exams (e.g. Alice may be more talented or hard-working than Sarah, for example; or Alice may have had better training than Sarah, or better studying opportunities than Sarah, and so on). That only empirically adequate theories survive does not begin to show why theory *X* (rather than theory *Y*) has got what it takes to survive – the realist would reply to van Fraassen. What we want to know is what makes theory *X* (but not *Y*) survival-adaptive. And here it seems we have to fall back on realism again in saying that *X* is survival-adaptive because it is ultimately true, because what the theory says about both observable *and unobservable entities* is true. The ability to save the phenomena, as a survival-adaptive criterion, must be ultimately traceable back to the theory being true (how would it otherwise be able to save the phenomena if not by a miracle or lucky happenstance?). Thus, one may contend, van Fraassen's Darwinian gloss on the no-miracles argument does not rule out scientific realism.

The second rejoinder attacks van Fraassen's distinction between observables and unobservables, by noting that the inferential path that leads to unobservables is one and the same path that leads to unobserved observables. Consider the many ways in which an object, otherwise perfectly observable under van Fraassen's criterion for observability (i.e. by the naked eye) may nonetheless go unobserved (Churchland's paper in Churchland and Hooker 1985). Sometimes objects may go unobserved because (A) they are too far away in time (in the Jurassic period, say) or too far away in space (in the Andromeda galaxy). Or they may go unobserved because (B) they are too small (e.g. neutrinos) or too feeble to be detected (e.g. cosmic background radiation as evidence for the Big Bang). What makes objects that fall under (A) distinct from objects that fall under (B)? The realist would insist that there is not a sufficient ground, even within van Fraassen's own resources, to draw a clear-cut distinction between (A)-cases and (B)-cases. In particular, the realist would insist that the way we come to *infer* the existence of objects, which though perfectly observable may nonetheless go unobserved because of (A), e.g. dinosaurs in the Jurassic period, or stars in the Andromeda galaxy, is exactly the *same way* in which we come to infer the existence of objects, which are unobservable because of (B) e.g. neutrinos and cosmic background radiation.

Consider dinosaurs in the Jurassic period, or marine extinct species such as trilobites in the Paleozoic era. None of us has ever seen either a dinosaur or a trilobite. Yet we believe that there was a historical period where dinosaurs and trilobites populated the globe because palaeontologists have accumulated enough fossil evidence to be able to reconstruct the skeletons and make inferences about the life, eating habits and even the cause of extinction of these animals. But as fossils provide evidence for now-extinct species, similarly, one can argue neutrino detectors provide evidence for neutrinos and the Large Hadron Collider provides evidence for the Higgs boson, and so forth. The inferential path that leads to the unobservable neutrino or Higgs boson is one and the same inferential path that leads to unobserved observable trilobites or dinosaurs. This inferential path has the name of **inference to the best explanation** (or IBE).

According to this pattern of inference, we infer the hypothesis which would, if true, provide the best explanation of the available evidence (Lipton 2004). Thus, we infer the existence of marine arthropods like trilobites because this is the best explanation for fossil evidence. Similarly, we infer the Higgs boson as the best explanation for the evidence coming from the Large Hadron Collider. In each case, we choose from a pool of competing explanatory hypotheses the one that we regard as the best, namely the one that – if true – would provide a deeper understanding of the available evidence. Inference to the best explanation is a very powerful tool in everyday life (when we infer that a mouse must be living in the kitchen as the best explanation for the crumbs on the floor disappearing) as well as in medical diagnostics, and science at large. Scientific realists appeal to this type of inference to reply to van Fraassen that we have reasons for believing in unobservable entities (no less than in observable ones) as the best explanation for the available evidence, and as such no compelling argument can be found for confining our beliefs to observable phenomena only.

The debate between scientific realists and constructive empiricists has left a profound mark in the philosophy of science of the past thirty years. Some philosophers feel that the debate has reached a standstill and that new forms of realism need to be explored to address the aforementioned challenges. It goes beyond the scope of this chapter to examine the current available alternatives. What I hope to have conveyed is that

debates about the aims of science have been central to the development
of our scientific history, and continue to be the source of inspiration for
contemporary philosophers of science.

Chapter summary

- Philosophy of science is the branch of philosophy that deals
  with conceptual problems and foundational issues arising from
  science.
- An important and ongoing debate in philosophy of science concerns
  the aim of science: what is science all about? What is the goal of
  scientific inquiry? We have identified two main traditions within this
  debate: scientific realism and antirealism.
- Scientific realism takes truth as the ultimate goal of science. Scientists aim to offer theories, which, once literally construed, we believe
  to be true. We identified three main aspects in the definition of
  scientific realism: a metaphysical aspect, a semantic aspect and an
  epistemic one.
- The main argument for scientific realism is the no-miracles argument,
  which says that scientific realism is the only philosophy that does
  not make the success of science a miracle or a lucky coincidence.
- We identified different varieties of antirealism, depending on which
  of the three aforementioned aspects in the definition of scientific
  realism is played down. We focused our attention on one variety,
  known as constructive empiricism.
- Constructive empiricism takes empirical adequacy (rather than
  truth) as the ultimate goal of science. A scientific theory is empirically adequate if what it says about observable things and events in
  the world is true. In other words, a theory is empirically adequate if
  it saves the phenomena.
- In the name of empirical adequacy as the final aim of science, constructive empiricism enjoins us to suspend belief about unobservable
  entities (e.g. neutrinos, DNA strands, etc.) on the ground that we do
  not need to believe in them to explain the success of science and we
  can instead offer a 'Darwinian' explanation for it (*pace* the realist
  no-miracles argument).
- Finally, we considered two realist responses against constructive
  empiricism. The first challenges the Darwinian reformulation of the
  no-miracles argument. The second invokes inference to the best
  explanation as the distinctive inferential path that leads to beliefs in
  unobservable entities no less than in unobserved observables, like
  dinosaurs and trilobites.

Study questions

1 Explain, in your own words, what the aims of science might be, and give an example of each taken from the history of science.
2 What is scientific realism? What is involved in embracing a realist view of science?
3 Consider the metaphysical aspect in the definition of scientific realism. Can you explain in your own words why we must think of the objects of scientific inquiry as being mind-independent?
4 Recall the semantic aspect in the definition of scientific realism. What is a theoretical term? And what does the expression 'construing the language of science literally' mean?
5 Coming to the epistemic aspect in the definition of scientific realism, when is a scientific theory true, or approximately true?
6 What is constructive empiricism? Why is it an antirealist position?
7 How does constructive empiricism define 'empirical adequacy'? What counts as 'observable phenomena'?
8 How can a constructive empiricist explain the success of science? Can you think of any example that may illustrate this point?
9 How compelling do you find the distinction between observable and unobservable? How can it be defended?
10 What is inference to the best explanation? How does it work in the debate between realists and constructive empiricists?

Introductory further reading

Ladyman, J. (2002) *Understanding Philosophy of Science,* New York: Routledge. (This is a very good introduction to philosophy of science, and it covers scientific realism in chapter 5.)
Putnam, H. (1978) 'What Is Realism?', in *Meaning and the Moral Sciences,* London: Routledge. (Here you find the classical statement of scientific realism and of the no-miracles argument.)
Psillos, S. (1999) *Scientific Realism: How Science Tracks Truth,* London: Routledge. (This is a very informative monograph on scientific realism. See chapter 4 for a defence of scientific realism; and chapter 9, for a critical discussion of constructive empiricism.)
van Fraassen, Bas (1980) *The Scientific Image,* Oxford: Clarendon. (This monograph is a classic in this debate. See especially, chapter 2 for a criticism of scientific realism; and chapter 3, for the positive statement of constructive empiricism.)

Advanced further reading

Churchland, P. and Hooker, C. A. (eds) (1985) *Images of Science,* Chicago: University of Chicago Press. (This is one of the first extensive anthologies of critical essays on constructive empiricism, with a long reply by van Fraassen.)

Duhem, P. (1908/1969) *To Save the Phenomena: An Essay on the Idea of Physical Theory from Plato to Galileo*, trans. E. Dolan, Chicago: University of Chicago Press. (This is a great little book, which reconstructs the history of the empiricist tradition of saving the phenomena from the Greek times to Galileo.)

Kitcher, P. (1993) *The Advancement of Science*, New York: Oxford University Press. (This is a more advanced monograph in defence of scientific realism. See in particular chapter 5.)

Lipton, P. (2004) *Inference to the Best Explanation*, 2nd edn, London: Routledge. (This book is a lucid and crisp defence of inference to the best explanation. See especially chapters 4 and 9.)

Monton, B. (ed.) (2007) *Images of Empiricism*, New York: Oxford University Press. (A great anthology of more recent essays on van Fraassen's constructive empiricism, with a reply by van Fraassen himself.)

Morgan, M. and Morrison, M. (1999) *Models as Mediators*, Cambridge: Cambridge University Press. (A must-read if you want to get started on the topic of scientific models and how they work in science.)

Internet resources

Chakravartty, A. (2011) 'Scientific Realism', in E. Zalta (ed.) *Stanford Encyclopedia of Philosophy* [online encyclopedia] http://plato.stanford.edu/entries/scientific-realism/.

Frigg, R. and Hartmann, S. (2012) 'Models in Science', in E. Zalta (ed.) *Stanford Encyclopedia of Philosophy* [online encyclopedia] http://plato.stanford.edu/entries/models-science/.

Monton, B. and Mohler, C. (2012) 'Constructive Empiricism', *Stanford Encyclopaedia of Philosophy* [online encyclopedia], http://plato.stanford.edu/entries/constructive-empiricism/.

7   Time travel and metaphysics

Alasdair Richmond

Introduction – why philosophy of time travel?

One of the central topics of philosophy is metaphysics, where we investigate the fundamental nature of reality and related questions. One good way to begin to understand some of the central issues of metaphysics is to consider a topic which is interesting, wide-ranging and growing in popularity. So why **time travel** particularly? Well, there is an extensive (and fascinating) range of metaphysical issues centred on time: for example, questions concerning persistence and identity over time, the passage of time and even whether or not time actually exists. However, this chapter tackles a topic that might allow you to see how philosophers tackle an issue in metaphysics using logical analysis, and an issue that has plenty of potential for interaction with science too, namely the philosophy of time travel. It's also the case that, odd as it sounds, where I might be hard put to it to offer a snappy, one-line definition of time itself, thanks to the work of American philosopher **David Lewis** (1941–2001), I can offer you a pretty snappy definition of time *travel*. (See below …)

Time travel, whether as a source of problems in logic, metaphysics or physics, raises some serious, deep and seriously deep questions. The definition of time travel we'll work with throughout comes from a philosopher (the aforesaid David Lewis), but it is a definition which is underwritten by physics just as much as by philosophy. Considering the topic of time travel might help guide our understanding of time, space, causation, identity and freedom, to say nothing of physical laws, computation, cosmology and the status of the past.

So let me stress at the outset that our topic is travelling to other times whether in the future or the past. Might such a thing be possible? If not, why not? If time travel were possible, what might that imply about time, freedom and even our selves? But before tackling those questions, let's first consider this question:

What is time travel?

The best and most famous philosophical paper about time travel to date is David Lewis's 'The Paradoxes of Time Travel'. David Lewis believed that it is logically possible to travel in time – forward or backward. What does that mean? Lewis argued that some time-travel journeys can be described without contradictions – that (to put it another way) time travel might take place in a possible world. (Maybe only a very strange world though – a world that differs from the world we think we live in in lots of ways.)

Please note that claiming that time travel is logically possible is not at all the same thing as claiming that time travel is physically possible – still less is it to claim that time travel is actually going on. This is an important point because Lewis's argument does not carry any commitment at all to time travel being physically possible or technologically possible or actual. One might accept Lewis's arguments and yet believe that time travel cannot occur. As Lewis emphasizes, a time-travel world, even if possible, might be very unlike our world.

It's still a remarkable thing if time travel is logically possible. Showing that something is logically contradictory is a very powerful weapon in the philosopher's armoury – it's one thing to make a claim which is merely factually wrong but it's quite another to fall into contradiction.

Lewis offers this very helpful definition of time travel:

> What is time travel? Inevitably, it involves discrepancy between time and time. Any traveler departs and then arrives at his destination; the time elapsed from departure to arrival (positive, or perhaps zero) is the duration of the journey. But if he is a time traveler, the separation in time between departure and arrival does not equal the duration of the journey.
>
> (1976: 145)

So, on Lewis's definition, time travel requires a distinction between two ways of registering time – what we will call **personal time** and **external time**.

Personal time is time as registered by the travelling object and should therefore reflect changes in all processes travelling with the object. So a traveller's watch, accumulating memories, greying hairs, digestive processes, cellular decay (etc.) might all be registers of personal time. Please note though: 'personal time' does *not* mean that only people can time travel. The gradual rusting of a time-travelling iron bucket would be just as good a register of personal time as any other. Moreover, time travel only occurs if *all* processes travelling with our voyager are affected – one does *not* become a time traveller simply by sleeping, hibernating or breaking one's watch. So hopping across time zones does not count as time travel – any more than breaking your watch or making its hands turn backward counts as time travel. (After all, time zones and watch-settings are conventional and artificial.)

External time on the other hand is time registered in the world at large – by such processes as (e.g.) the movement of the tides, the Earth's rotation, the Earth orbiting the sun, the recession of the galaxies, etc.

So, Lewis's claim is that, given a distinction between external time and personal time, it is at least possible to imagine **forward time travel** and **backward time travel**. Now here's the crucial bit: if you are not a time traveller, any journey you take will have the same duration and direction in personal time and in external time. However, if you are a time traveller, your journey will be different viewed in personal time or in external time.

A time-travel journey has different durations and/or different directions in external and personal time.

Note that the time traveller's ageing, memory traces (etc.) will vary with the traveller's personal time and not external time, so if you travelled to (e.g.) an external time after your death or one before your birth, you would not thereby cease to exist on arrival. So you can (in theory) be present at *external* times before you were born. What you can't do however is to be present at a *personal* time before you were born.

For forward time travellers, the journey's personal time has the same direction as external time but different duration. Suppose I travel from 2013 to 2163 in five minutes of personal time as measured by (e.g.) my watch and my memories. Then, by Lewis's definition, I have time travelled into the future – my journey takes five minutes in personal time but 150 years in external time. Importantly, the possibility of forward time travel seems to be a very deeply embedded phenomenon in one of our best-supported physical theories. Einstein's 1905 special theory of relativity predicts that such phenomena actually occur. To test such 'time dilation' experimentally, physicists measure the decay half-life of a particle at rest (e.g. a π-meson) and then see how long it takes to decay when at high speed. Decay-times lengthen with velocity just as special relativity predicts.

Now, if I'm lucky, I maybe have 40 or even 50 years of personal time ahead of me. Special relativity says that if I travel fast enough relative to the solar system, I can make that 40- or 50-year interval of personal time comprise tens or hundreds or millions or even billions of years of external time. Indeed, provided that I travel fast enough, I can make my 40 years of personal time extend through the entire future history of the sun. So forward time travel is very deeply embedded in Einstein's special relativity and decades of well-supported physical results suggest these durational divergences really occur.

For backward time travellers, the journey has *different directions* in personal and external time. Suppose I travel for five minutes of personal time but from 2013 to 1863. Here, my journey has positive personal duration (so it ends after it begins for me) but negative external duration – my journey ends 150 external years *before* it begins. Such directional discrepancy between personal and external time would make me a backward time traveller.

Backward time travel is more speculative, and whether physics permits backward time travel is still hotly contested. Einstein's 1918 general theory of relativity seems to predict that under certain circumstances (given an enormous amount of mass or an enormous density of mass or enormously rapid movement of mass), it's possible to create circumstances where personal time and external time diverge not only in duration but in direction, i.e. allowing backward time travel. In 1949, Austrian logician and mathematical physicist **Kurt Gödel** (1903–78) used the general theory of relativity to describe a world where it's possible to travel between any points in space and time. So the general theory seems to underwrite the kind of personal-time/external-time discrepancies that are constitutive of backward time travel as well. Quantum mechanics too may allow backward time travel. However, either way it doesn't look easy and the prospects for practical backward time travel are not looking bright as of 27 May 2013. (Sorry if anyone is disappointed by that outcome – I know I am – but I stress this is philosophy of time travel and not a guide to building time machines.)

Given the personal/external-time distinction, we've passed the first hurdle en route to seeing why time travel might be logically possible. The main focus from now on is on backward time travel. Why might backward time travel seem to present logical problems? How might these problems be addressed? These questions bring us to …

Grandfather paradoxes

The classic argument against the logical possibility of time travel appeals to the **grandfather paradox**. If you could travel backward in time, you could (supposedly) travel back to a time before one of your grandfathers became a parent and assassinate him, thereby preventing one of your parents from existing and hence preventing yourself from being born. So if your mission succeeded, you would not be there to carry out your mission. Paradox ahoy. One and the same person cannot both exist and not exist at the same time. (Like Lewis and most other philosophers, we will assume reality must be consistent and that no existing thing can truly be described in contradictions.)

So the classic argument against backward time travel runs something like this:

Premise 1. If it is possible to travel backwards in time, it is possible to create contradictory states of affairs.
Premise 2. It is not possible to create contradictory states of affairs.
Conclusion. Therefore, it is not possible to travel backwards in time.

This argument is valid. It has the classic logical form 'modus tollens': 'If *P* then *Q*; not *Q*; therefore not *P*'. *Logically* the argument is impeccable. However, an argument guarantees the truth of its conclusion only if it is not merely *valid* but *sound*, i.e. it is a valid argument that contains only true premises. But is the above a sound argument? Lewis says 'No.'

Lewis would accept the validity of the above argument but he would deny its soundness on the grounds that one premise is false. In particular, Lewis's claim is that while premise 1 is true, premise 2 is not true, and therefore the argument has not proved its conclusion to be true. While Lewis did believe that it is impossible to create contradictory states of affairs, he did not accept that being able to travel backward in time would make it possible to create contradictory states of affairs.

Central to Lewis's argument is the claim that the above argument needs to be unambiguous about what 'possible' means and, as Lewis emphasizes, the term 'possible' can mean different things according to context. Here we need to do a spot of logical analysis on the notion of possibility and try to unpack the different ways in which something can be said to be possible. Lewis argues that confusion follows if the different senses of possibility are not kept clearly distinguished and that the grandfather paradox argument is guilty of precisely such confusion.

In order to assess what time travellers in the past (or indeed anyone else) can and cannot do, we need to be very clear about what sense of possibility we have in mind, and, in particular, we need to consider what might be possible relative to a given set of facts. So where does the appearance of paradox come from? Why does the grandfather paradox argument have such an appeal? And Lewis says it's because there's an ambiguity, or worse than an ambiguity, in the argument's very first premise: 'If it is possible to travel backward in time, it is possible to generate paradoxes.' Well, what does 'possible' mean? Lewis says that to answer this question properly, we need the notion of something being *compossible*.

Philosophers sometimes talk about **compossibility**, meaning by that possibility relative to some states of affairs, facts or circumstances. This notion of compossibility is originally due to Gottfried Wilhelm Leibniz (1646–1716). Lewis writes, 'To say that something can happen means that its happening is compossible with certain facts. Which facts? That is determined, but sometimes not determined well enough, by context' (1976: 143).

As a thought experiment, consider the following: I don't have a problem with either of my (sadly late) grandfathers so for purposes of discussion, assume I am on a mission to remove from history somebody I do have a problem with, namely Adolf Hitler (1889–1945). Let's assume I travel from 2013 on a mission to assassinate Hitler in Vienna in 1908. I've done my homework and I think this juncture in history presents the best chances of success, i.e. Hitler's so-called 'hunger years' when he was eking out a living as an artist in Vienna. So I activate my machine and thereafter later moments of my personal time unfold in earlier external times – specifically in 1908.

(As an aside: lest all this talk of assassination seem a shade too violent, please feel free to imagine I'm on some less bloodthirsty mission to the past, e.g. trying to make a paradoxical change in history by buying up Hitler's paintings and getting him to live out the rest of his life as a mediocre landscape artist. Preventing Hitler's actual career as Führer thus would involve just as much of a contradiction with recorded history as actually assassinating him. Please note that paradoxes do not come in sizes – so any such changes to actual history cannot be 'slightly' paradoxical or 'a bit' paradoxical.)

Let's suppose I can travel from 2013 to Vienna in 1908. Can my mission succeed? Well, what counts as possibility varies with the set of facts considered. There are some facts about the Vienna 1908 set-up which are compossible with success, e.g. Hitler isn't bulletproof, my gun is working. However, including a bigger, more inclusive set of facts brings in other facts which are definitely not compossible with my succeeding, e.g. my target doesn't die until 1945. Assuming death is a one-off operation, I cannot kill in 1908 someone who dies in 1945. But, importantly:

My being unable to succeed is not the same thing as my being unable to try.

On Lewis's analysis, backward time travel is consistent (i.e. logically possible) if the consequences of a traveller's actions are in place in the history whence the traveller departs. So I can (logically at least) travel from 2013 to 1908 provided that everything I do in 1908 is consistent with the history whence I come.

So I can't do anything in 1908 that hasn't already happened in the history whence I come. If I get Hitler in my sights in 1908, there seems a guarantee of failure. But that failure might take any one of a number of forms. My gun could jam, I could sneeze, Hitler could duck to tie up his shoelaces, I could be run over by a tram – *or* I could successfully shoot down somebody I believe is Hitler, only to discover I've shot the wrong person.

A non-time-travel example (adapted from Lewis): can I speak (Scots) Gaelic? In one sense, I can: I have 'got what it takes' in so far as I currently have a functioning larynx and have learned at least one language. But don't ask me for a recitation of any of Scotland's rich heritage of Gaelic verse because in another, more inclusive, sense, I can't speak Gaelic – alas I simply never learned enough of the words or the grammar. My speaking Gaelic is compossible with some facts about me but not with a more inclusive set. However there's no paradox here because the relevant senses of possibility vary according to the facts considered.

Another example: can I stop smoking? Well, in a sense, I can – relative to facts like: there are various support groups for people trying to quit smoking, various nicotine substitutes exist and I flatter myself I am not totally devoid of will power. So far, so compossible with my stopping smoking. But there's a *logical* problem with my stopping smoking: I can't *stop* smoking because as it happens I don't smoke. (And my smoking is a logical precondition for my being able to stop smoking.) But stopping smoking per se is logically perfectly okay and is also compossible with many facts about me – although (crucially) not all of them.

One more example – suppose you try to construct a *Euclidean* triangle with sides of the following lengths: 3 centimetres, 4 centimetres and 5 centimetres. That is logically entirely possible, if maybe difficult to achieve perfectly in practice in a lumpy, bumpy world like ours. However, not physical restrictions but rather *logic* forbids you constructing a Euclidean triangle with sides of these lengths: 3 centimetres, 4 centimetres and 500 kilometres. The third length of side cannot be combined with both of the other two in a Euclidean triangle. But there's nothing logically funny about triangles. The triangle-making task would be logically achievable given any two of the three lengths of side above but alas, success is not compossible with all three of the assigned sides taken jointly.

Lewis thinks backward time travel is logically possible even if there is only one history. (I'll mention many-histories time travel later on.) Again, this is not the same thing as claiming that backward time travel is *physically possible* in a single history. Maybe single-history backward travel is logically possible but physically impossible. (As we'll learn, some people have argued for something very like this conclusion.)

What this means is that in Lewis's model, backward time travel is still logically possible provided each moment in history happens only once. Backward time travel does not require one and the same moment to happen repeatedly or to happen in different parallel versions – as if Vienna managed to get through 1908 without my presence and then (somehow) I travel back and make 1908 happen again, only differently with me there this time. Thinking that time travel must involve times happening 'again' is a (surprisingly common) mistake which has been dubbed by Nicholas J. J. Smith the 'second-time-around fallacy'.

Here's the thing: if travellers from the future (or the past) did not visit 1908 then there is nothing that later (or earlier) times can do to alter that fact. But then again, if future travellers were present in 1908 then nothing later (or earlier) times can possibly do could alter *that* fact either. (If they're there, they're there – if they're not, they're not. That last remark may sound obvious but its implications run deep.)

Well okay, you may be thinking, maybe backward time travel is logically possible provided the history the traveller arrives in is consistent with the history the traveller departs from. But Lewis's analysis *might* seem to suggest that a time traveller is completely impotent in the past – constrained merely to observe.

Worse, it might seem as if time travel only makes sense if the backward traveller is only present in the past as a totally impalpable ghost, unable to affect anything in the past whatsoever. But this 'ghost traveller' idea actually rests on another mistake …

Two senses of change

It might sound as if consistency demands that time travellers in the past must be utterly powerless. Or to put it another way, surely a time traveller can't change the past without creating paradoxes? Well, just as the notion of possibility needs to be unpacked to prevent ambiguity, so too does the notion of change. In one sense, a time traveller can change the past – or maybe more correctly, in one sense, a traveller can have an impact on the past.

Change is another term prone to ambiguity in ordinary contexts. To adapt a point from Lewis, consider what might be called **replacement change** and **counterfactual change**.

An example of replacement change: an intact glass drops onto a concrete floor and shatters. So the intact glass is replaced by a mass of glass shards. Concrete objects suffer replacement changes all the time. (I spill my coffee and a full mug is replaced by an empty one. I sneeze and a completed jigsaw is replaced by a mess of separate pieces. You finish your homework and an unfinished assignment is replaced by a completed one.) There's a phase of history with an intact glass and then a phase featuring a smashed glass. But please note that nowhere in history are the intact and smashed phases superimposed.

Consider now the slightly more rarefied-sounding but actually pretty familiar notion of counterfactual change. With counterfactual change, we assess the impact that something makes by considering how events would have unfolded if that something hadn't occurred. A counterfactual (sometimes written 'contrary-to-fact conditional') expresses a relationship of consequence by taking as antecedent something that didn't in fact happen – for example, 'If the internal combustion engine had not been invented, travel in the twentieth century would have been a lot slower.' (A more mundane example: if my alarm clock hadn't gone off at the correct time this morning, I would have slept in.)

Another example: it's widely agreed (not least by the Duke of Wellington) that the outcome of the Battle of Waterloo on 18 June 1815 was crucially affected by the arrival of a Prussian army under Field Marshall Blücher. Suppose it's true that without Blücher's intervention, the French forces would have triumphed. So we can assert the counterfactual conditional 'If Blücher had been delayed, Napoleon would have won.' Clearly Blücher's arrival had an impact, or to put it another way, Blücher's arrival changed the course of history. But changed *in what way*? Not by replacement – it isn't as if there was once a version of 18 June 1815 where Napoleon won at Waterloo and then Blücher's appearance (paradoxically) made the French victory go away so an allied victory could take its place. Waterloo happened only once, ending in an allied victory, but Blücher still changed its outcome.

Whither time travel in all this? Well, here's the important bit regarding change: Lewis thinks travellers in the past can only change history in the counterfactual sense, i.e. in the sense that history would have been different had the traveller not been present.

Lewis thinks travellers cannot make replacement changes in history. But, he says, *nobody* can make a replacement change to *any* moment in history, past, present or future. If I initially decide to have coffee with my lunch, only to change my mind and opt for peppermint tea, I have not thereby replaced an 'Alasdair has coffee' future with an 'Alasdair has peppermint tea' future. So replacement changes can happen to concrete objects but they cannot happen to times. Nonetheless, a time traveller in the past can make a counterfactual impact and thereby (in a very real and important sense) be said to have changed history. (Note, though, my killing Hitler in 1908 would be a replacement change, and therefore impossible.)

Okay, let's now try to construct a time-travel story whereby the traveller has a counterfactual (i.e. non-replacement) impact on history. Suppose my time machine arrives in 1908 Vienna so close to my target that my arrival causes Hitler to leap backward, out of the path of an oncoming tram that would otherwise have ended his life. In this case, I would have made an impact on history but definitely not the one I would have wanted – in other words, my impact could be assessed with the counterfactual 'If I hadn't travelled back in time, Hitler would have died in 1908.' So, if this sequence of events had played out, I would have been (albeit quite unwittingly and involuntarily) partly responsible for Hitler's rise to power. A very worrying thought for the aspirant time traveller ... maybe you can have an impact in the past but your impact may not be a beneficial one at all. Travellers need not visit the past as ghosts but as concrete, fully actual, living, breathing humans.

Another example: suppose now I travel back to 1863 and I bump into Lincoln. Lincoln is about to give the world-famous words of the Gettysburg address but he's unsure which version to give. He has a choice between the famous version that history records and another version. And I say to him 'Mr President, sir, if I might make a suggestion: go with the version that starts with these great resonant sentences about how this nation was conceived in liberty – believe me, that will go down very well.' And Lincoln takes my advice, and the other version of the speech is discarded. But suppose if I hadn't intervened, Lincoln would have recited a different version of the Gettysburg Address. Well, I've clearly had an impact on history – history is different as a result of my efforts. But I've not *replaced* anything – I've not made one version of the Gettysburg Address disappear and another version take its place. The Gettysburg Address happens once, and once only. But I've still changed the course of history.

So the lesson of these examples is that travellers in a single history can help to make the past what it was without generating paradoxes, provided their impact on past events is a counterfactual one and not one involving the replacement of past events.

A word of caution: when Lewis says: *all* the consequences of the traveller's actions are in place in the history whence the traveller comes, he really means absolutely *all* of the consequences whatsoever – every blade of grass trodden on, every flapping butterfly disturbed, every bacterium jostled, every light-reflectance deflected – the whole lot. So please note, Lewis is definitely *not* saying 'It's okay to (replacement-) change the past as long as you only change it a bit.' That (hopelessly illogical) answer is maybe okay for fiction but not for us – no replacement changes to any times, ever, anywhere in history, is the Lewis line. However, you can still affect (i.e. counterfactually change) the past.

At the risk of belabouring the point, please note that in Lewis's analysis, each moment is assumed to happen once and once only – whether or not there is a time traveller (or travellers) present. So again, your just being in (e.g.) 1908 need not make a replacement change in history. From the fact that you cannot change past events into something that they weren't, it doesn't follow that you therefore cannot have an impact in the past.

You may also be thinking: well how can something as abstract as logic *constrain* something as concrete as physical actions? Indeed, this is a good question but it may rest on a mistaken notion of constraint. Granted, it does seem weird to think of our actions as being under logical constraint but some examples might make it seem less bizarre. For example, you can't make a sphere bigger than itself or discover an even prime number bigger than two. Likewise, you can't trisect an angle using just an unmarked ruler and a compass. We may not feel under constraint in these cases and yet we cannot perform the tasks described. Then again, maybe logic doesn't so much constrain as just describe the most general rules that there are.

'But surely', I hear you cry, 'this does not exhaust the problems presented by backward time travel.' Indeed not. Which brings us to ...

Causal loops

There's another kind of time travel example that poses problems that don't involve consistency but rather information and specifically the origins of that information. The cases in question involve what we'll call **causal loops**.

A causal loop is an unusual kind of causal chain, namely a chain of events which loops backwards in time so that an event proves to be among its own causes. (Note this is not the same as a positive feedback loop, which involves normal causation throughout.) In a causal loop, an event turns out to be (at least in part) a cause of itself. Philosophers have often felt that such loops are philosophically intolerable. Perhaps unsurprisingly, Lewis disagrees ... A couple of examples of causal loops:

Imagine you travel back in time to 1588 equipped with a copy of Shakespeare's complete works printed in 2013. On arrival, you meet struggling young player, Will Shaxberd (as he was *maybe* then calling himself), and you read Will the following lines:

What a piece of work is a man,
How noble in reason,
How infinite in faculty,
In form and moving, how express and admirable ...

In short, you read Will a great soliloquy from *Hamlet*. (Specifically, from *Hamlet*, Act II, scene 2.) You then let Will copy all the contents of the *Complete Works* you've brought with you. Shaxberd (as was) duly arranges for his manuscript copies to be circulated to Elizabethan stage-companies (maybe changing his name to the more familiar 'Shakespeare' en route). The plays become popular, pass into the canon of British drama and are reprinted until you obtain a *Complete Works* in 2013, which you take back to 1588 ...

Now there seems to be no inconsistency here – no grandfather paradoxes or 'replacement changes' involved – yet there is something odd nonetheless. Even if this case is consistent, one might ask: but where does the information come from? Or to put it another way, who wrote *Hamlet* in this imagined example?

Here's another example (freely adapted from Lewis 1976): you're sitting at home one evening when the telephone rings. You pick up the telephone and answer it, to hear an oddly familiar voice saying 'Don't say a word. Write these instructions down and follow them to the letter.' The instructions prove to be for building and operating a time machine.

You follow the instructions and the machine takes you into the recent past. On arrival, you dial your own phone number and, when an oddly familiar voice answers, you say into the receiver 'Don't say a word. Write these instructions down and follow them to the letter' ...

This story, even if we grant that it is consistent, prompts the question: How do you know how to build a time machine? Well, your later self knows how because you remember hearing the instructions as your earlier self. In turn, your earlier self knows how because of remembering being instructed by your later self. But where does the information come from in the first place? Perhaps surprisingly, Lewis's answer is: there is no answer. He says:

His earlier self knew how because his older self had been told and the information had been preserved by the causal processes that constitute telling. But where did the information come from in the first place? Why did the whole affair happen? There is simply no answer. The parts of the loop are explicable, the whole of it is not.

(1976: 140)

The instructions for building a time machine in Lewis's case (or in the *Hamlet* case as above), in a real sense do not 'come from' anywhere – they simply are. Causal loops appear strange but are no worse from the point of view of ultimate explanation than any other kind of causal chain.

We have no complete explanation for any causal sequence (closed or linear) and we may just have to accept spontaneous creation of information in other cases. Explaining the existence of the whole loop may be a very different matter from explaining the existence of any loop component. There seem to be only three possible forms a causal chain could take:

(1) Finite linear – causal chains that terminate in events that are causes but that do not themselves have causes.
(2) Infinite linear – each event has a cause, and those causes in turn have causes, and so on ad infinitum. The chain as a whole has no beginning.
(3) Finite non-linear – the chain loops back on itself.

In the first case, we can only take the analysis of our chain back so far before we hit an event that is a cause but that itself has no prior cause. Physicists take very seriously the idea that there are such *ex nihilo* happenings, e.g. the emission of alpha particles or even the Big Bang that brought this universe into existence. The chain itself has no prior cause for its existence and taken as a whole appears inexplicable. (As Stephen Hawking put it, asking what came before the Big Bang is like asking what lies to the north of the North Pole. If you try heading north at the North Pole, you find yourself heading south.)

In the second case, we can pursue the chain of causes literally infinitely (i.e. every event has a cause distinct from itself stretching back forever) and never arrive at an 'unmoved mover' or 'uncaused causer' so again the occurrence of the whole chain is without explanation.

In the third case, the search for an earlier explanatory event leads right the way round the chain to the very event we started from. Again there is no explanation of the whole chain.

So Lewis does not try to address the causal loop problem by trying to explain where the information comes from. Instead, he offers a parity argument: granted there is no well-formed explanation for the existence of a causal loop taken in its entirety. However, exactly the same can be urged in the case of linear causal chains (finite or infinite).

On the face of it, this 'no answer' answer of Lewis's isn't very satisfactory. Surely we have stories for the origins of information and information just doesn't spring into being from nothing? Well, it's important to distinguish between asking where an *event* comes from and asking where *an entire chain of events comes from*. The first question is perfectly sensible but the second maybe less so. When it comes to explaining an event, we can usually appeal to some earlier event. I am alive now in part because of facts about my parents. Those facts in turn reflect facts about human evolution, the origins of the Milky Way and the history of the universe ... But where does the whole chain come from? Lewis's point is that all three kinds of chain are equally mysterious when it comes to their ultimate origin. Ultimately, a causal loop is no more (or less) hard to explain than any other kind of causal chain.

Another way to look at Lewis's point might go something like this: we have very good explanatory tools for giving an account of where individual events come from – but it's rather less clear that we have any handle on explaining ultimately where an entire causal chain comes from, regardless of the way in which that chain is structured. While it makes sense to ask why a given event occurred, it's much less clear that it makes sense to ask where entire causal chains ultimately come from.

Where next?

There are lots of philosophical time travel questions we haven't covered. Here are brief mentions of a few:

(1) Time travel poses some interesting problems in persistence and identity. Consider the Lewis telephone call case again: here, we seemingly have two versions of the same person existing in different places at the same (external) time. Concrete objects (like people) presumably cannot be completely located in more than one place at a time. How might time travel confer the apparent power of bilocation?

(2) Lots of interesting philosophical questions arise from the physics of time travel. What sort of physical laws might occur in a world that permitted time travel? Physicist David Deutsch argues that

physically realistic time travel can only occur if there are many histories. Deutsch argues thus: backward-travelling systems face curious restrictions on their actions. In time-travel contexts, otherwise physically possible set-ups seem to yield impossible outcomes. (Guns that should normally be able to kill unarmoured people seem to fail of their normal function, etc.) This argument appeals to something like an 'autonomy principle': the causal powers of a physical system should reflect only local facts about that system and should not depend on the state of the universe as a whole.

Deutsch thinks a backward time traveller at a given space-time locale in a single-world system would not have the same causal powers as an arbitrarily similar but non-time-travelling individual at the same location. In other words, if a locally based agent in 1908 could have shot Hitler dead, then so could a (sufficiently similar) time traveller in 1908 who hails from 2013. So a way to avoid weird-looking constraints on time travellers in the past would be for the travellers to be translated into a distinct branch or history. Therefore, Deutsch argues, the only way to keep time travel physically realistic is to imagine that backward time travellers must also make a transition into an alternative world or different branch of history. So I could travel to (one version of) 1908 and kill Hitler – the Hitler I kill resides in one branch and the Hitler from my history resides in another. No paradox because the Hitler who dies in 1908 and the one who dies in 1945 are distinct individuals in different branches.

So you could have your full freedom of action, without generating paradoxes, at the cost of accepting the existence of many worlds. But interesting questions remain:

Does 'many worlds time travel' really qualify as time travel? You might feel that if your destination is in a different history, you haven't really travelled in time.

(3) Stephen Hawking asked 'If time travel is possible, where are the time travellers?' In a similar spirit, some philosophers have argued that if backward time travel did occur, we would know about it because time travellers from the future would trail long chains of unlikely coincidences in their wakes. Suppose I go back in time to the end of 1908 with a bus full of assassins, and we each take a separate mechanism for trying to whack Hitler. Somebody has a machine gun, someone has a bazooka, someone else has a poisoned hat, someone else has an exploding cake. And we all converge on Hitler's known history with our various infernal devices. No

matter how many times we try, we're guaranteed to fail. And surely if backward time travel occurred, we would see trails of unlikely coincidences, as people try to make replacement changes in history – and fail. But maybe only very unreflective travellers would keep trying to assassinate the famous ... and so unlikely output coincidences only follow from unlikely inputs.

(4) At the moment, one interesting line of approach holds that it might be possible to construct a realistic time machine, but at the cost that you couldn't control it. You could set up the conditions necessary to generate divergences between personal time and external time, but it would be physically impossible to predict what that mechanism would actually create. So you could set up a time machine, you could create a region of the universe where time travel occurred, and yet not be able to predict what sort of out-comes were generated by it. So (ironically) even if physics allows the construction of a time machine, it might not allow the device to be controllable ...

(5) When physicists discuss time travel, they often talk about **closed timelike curves** (CTCs). A CTC is a path through space-time that returns to the very point whence it departed but which never exceeds the speed of light along the way. So a CTC represents a physically possible pathway into the past. Might CTCs exist in the real world or something like it?

As above, Kurt Gödel in 1949 described a model universe using Einstein's general theory of relativity which is infinite, rotating (in a technical sense) and has CTCs through its every point. In a Gödel universe, all of space and time is accessible. Alas, Gödel's infinite, rotating, non-expanding universe is rather unlike our apparently finite, non-rotating and expanding universe.

However, it remains unclear whether the unification of general relativity and quantum mechanics (the long-sought theory of 'quantum gravity') will allow CTCs. Hawking's 'Where are the travellers?' problem threatens some scenarios more than others. If our universe were an infinite Gödel universe, the observed absence of time travellers might be very puzzling. However, physicists also discuss localized CTC-generators, i.e. ways to make CTC-regions in otherwise normal space-times. One thing that physicists are agreed on is that a CTC-generator is not a vehicle but a *region*: a region of curved space-time. Local CTC-devices all have the feature that they facilitate access to the past only from the first moment when a CTC is first generated. Sup-pose the first CTC-generator ever made comes online in 2015 – later times could use the CTC-generator to travel back to 2015 but no times before that could be accessed. Any CTC generator will only allow access to history over the period over which it itself exists. So maybe one answer to Hawking's question is that time travel is possible but not just yet ...

There are a host of metaphysical issues that space does not allow us to cover here. However, the possibility of time travel would affect our thinking in many different areas. For one thing, time travel would affect our ideas about the status of the past and the future. If other times can be visited then presumably those times must exist. This in turn would affect our ideas about free will. If the future exists, can it truly be open? But if the future isn't open, what happens to our freedom? If our future actions in some sense are already 'out there' can we really be said to be free? For another thing, what would laws of nature be like in a time-travel world? According to David Lewis, backward time travel is possible in a single history provided that the traveller's actions are consistent with the history whence the traveller comes. But what ensures that only consistency-preserving actions occur? Must a time-travel world have strange physical laws?

Chapter summary

- Time travel is defined by David Lewis as involving a discrepancy between personal time (time for the traveller) and external time (time in the outside world). In forward time travel, personal time and external time share the same direction but differ in duration. In backward time travel, personal time and external time differ in direction.

- The grandfather paradox argument against backward time travel says: if it is possible to travel backwards in time then it is possible to create contradictions. However, because it isn't possible to create contradictions, backward time travel is not possible. Lewis thinks this argument is valid but unsound.

- Lewis thinks the grandfather paradox argument fails because it treats possibility as unambiguous. In fact, possibility can mean different things in different contexts. Relative to some facts, you can assassinate grandfather but relative to others, you cannot.

- Lewis also thinks time travellers can have an impact on the past but only in a counterfactual sense and not a repayment sense. Time travellers can make the past different from what it would have been had they not been there – but they cannot replace one time with another one.

- Lewis considers causal loops – cases where a chain of events loops back in time so an event can be among its own causes. He thinks such cases are very odd but not impossible. Causal loops appear strange because we have no answer to the question of where they come from – but, Lewis says, we have no good answer to where any chain of events ultimately comes from.

Study questions

1 How does David Lewis define time travel?
2 What might forward time travel involve, on Lewis's definition?
3 And then again, what might backward time travel involve, on Lewis's definition?
4 If I could travel backward in time, could I assassinate myself as a baby?
5 What is the grandfather paradox argument supposed to show?
6 How did David Lewis try to show that time travel was logically possible?
7 What is 'compossibility' and how does Lewis apply the notion of compossibility to time-travel cases?
8 What are causal loops and what might be wrong with them?
9 How does Lewis try to defuse worries about causal loops?
10 Where does the information in a causal loop come from?
11 If a traveller goes back in time and meets her earlier self, has she become two people in so doing? If not, why not?
12 Would a traveller in the past be able to behave like a normal human agent or would she face strange constraints on her actions?

Introductory further reading

Dainton, B. (2010) *Time and Space*, 2nd edn, Durham: Acumen. (Offers by far the best available introduction to problems of time and space. Chapter 8 deals very thoroughly with time travel.)
Dowe, P. (2000) 'The Case for Time Travel', *Philosophy* 75: 441–51. (Detailed reply to Grey (1999) that tries to defuse and address all the problems hitherto alleged against time travel.)
Grey, W. (1999) 'Troubles with Time Travel', *Philosophy* 74: 55–70. (A handy summary of pretty much all the arguments that philosophers have mustered against the possibility of time travel so far.)
Nahin, P. (1999) *Time Machines: Time Travel in Physics, Metaphysics and Science Fiction*, 2nd edn, New York: American Institute of Physics. (Very thorough survey of time travel as treated in philosophy, science and science fiction. Very good on (e.g.) possible physical mechanisms for time travel.)

Richmond, A. (2001) 'Time-Travel Fictions and Philosophy', *American Philosophical Quarterly* 38: 305–18. (Surveys philosophical problems about time travel that arise in science fiction.)

Richmond, A. (2003) 'Recent Work: Time Travel', *Philosophical Books* 44: 297–309. (Outlines all the major philosophical works on time travel up to 2006.)

Smith, N. J. J. (1997) 'Bananas Enough for Time Travel?', *British Journal for the Philosophy of Science* 48: 363–89. (Argues thoroughly that backward time travel need not generate improbable coincidences and that even if it did, this would be no argument against backward time travel.)

Advanced further reading

Dwyer, L. (1975) 'Time Travel and Changing the Past', *Philosophical Studies* 27: 341–50. (A pre-Lewis argument that backward time travel may be logically possible after all.)

Gödel, K. (1949) 'An Example of a New Type of Cosmological Solutions of Einstein's Field Equations of Gravitation', *Reviews of Modern Physics* 21: 447–50. (Rather technical but very important: the first physical description of a time-travel universe.)

Lewis, D. (1976) 'The Paradoxes of Time Travel', *American Philosophical Quarterly* 13: 145–52, www.csus.edu/indiv/m/merlinos/Paradoxes%20of%20Time%20Travel.pdf. (The classic defence of the logical possibility of time travel and the best philosophical work on the topic bar none.)

Miller, K. (2006) 'Travelling in Time: How to Wholly Exist in Two Places at the Same Time', *Canadian Journal of Philosophy* 36: 309–34. (Interesting and lively attempt at explaining how time travel might allow a person to be in two places at the same time.)

Sorensen, R. (1987) 'Time Travel, Parahistory and Hume', *Philosophy* 62: 227–36. (Entertaining attempt at using time travel as a test case for Hume's argument concerning testimony to miracles.)

Vihvelin, K. (1996) 'What Time Travelers Cannot Do', *Philosophical Studies* 81: 315–30. (Interesting critique of problems of freedom facing the backward time traveller.)

Yourgrau, P. (1999) *Gödel Meets Einstein*, Chicago: Open Court. (Book-length defence of Gödel's fascinating argument that the possibility of closed timelike curves in Gödel universes shows that there is really no such thing as time.)

Internet resources

Arntzenius, F. and Maudlin, T. (2005) 'Time Travel and Modern Physics', in E. Zalta (ed.) *Stanford Encyclopedia of Philosophy* [online encyclopedia] (Summer 2005 edn), http://plato.stanford.edu/archives/sum2005/entries/time-travel-phys/. (Very thorough overview of the philosophy and physics of time travel.)

Carroll, J. W. (ed.) (2008) *A Time Travel Website*, http://timetravelphilosophy.net/. (Full to the brim of well-informed, nicely chosen and fun examples, arguments and references. Informative and comprehensive but entertaining too.)

Earman, J. and Wüthrich, C. (2004) 'Time Machines', in E. Zalta (ed.) *Stanford Encyclopedia of Philosophy* [online encyclopedia] (Fall 2008 edn), http://plato.stanford.edu/archives/fall2008/entries/time-machine/. (Thorough account of the feasibility of operating a time machine. Often technical.)

Hawking, S. (1999) 'Space and Time Warps', *Stephen Hawking* [website], www.hawking.org.uk/space-and-time-warps.html. (Accessible, popular and wide-ranging introduction to the fascinating problems and possibilities of curved space-time.)

Schwarz, P., *Time Travel in Flatland: An Animated Tutorial in Physics, Light Cones and Causality*, California Institute of Technology [website], no date, www.theory.caltech.edu/people/patricia/lctoc.html. (Unreservedly brilliant: splendid introduction to the physics and dynamics of time travel. Fun, serious and serious fun.)

Glossary of key terms

ability knowledge Often referred to as 'know-how', since it involves knowing how to do something, such as ride a bike or swim. It is usually contrasted with **propositional knowledge**, which is knowledge of a **proposition**. The two types of knowledge are treated differently because, intuitively at least, one might know how to do something (e.g. swim) without having any relevant propositional knowledge (e.g. without knowing that you can swim, perhaps because you forgot that you could until you fell in the water). *See also* **propositional knowledge.**

argument In philosophy, an argument is a series of considerations put forward to support a particular conclusion.

autonomy One is autonomous when one determines one's own destiny, as opposed to having one's destiny determined by others or by external factors. One is intellectually autonomous when one thinks for oneself, as opposed to being told by others what to think.

backward time travel Any journey or process in which time has different directions considered in **personal time** and **external time** – for example, a journey which has positive personal duration but negative external duration.

Cartesian dualism The view, named after its founder René Descartes, that there are two kinds of substance. Minds are made of *immaterial substance*; bodies and everything else in the world are made of *material substance. See also* **immaterial/material substances.**

causal loop A kind of causal chain which manages to loop back in time so that an event can be one of its own causes.

classical account of knowledge According to the classical account, knowledge is defined as justified true belief. This view is often credited to

Plato, and is sometimes referred to as the 'tripartite' (i.e. three-part) account of knowledge. *See also* **Gettier cases.**

closed timelike curve A path through space-time that leads back to the very point in space and time that it began from, but which nowhere involves exceeding the speed of light. A physical path into the past.

compossibility The possibility of a given outcome assessed relative to some other fact or state of affairs. Compossible states of affairs can exist together but states of affairs that are not compossible cannot both exist. For example, my being able to stop smoking is compossible with my having the will power to quit but is not compossible with the fact I don't smoke.

conceptual relativism A variety of **scientific antirealism** denying that nature (and its objects and entities) exists mind-independently. It claims that our concepts or conceptual schemes play an active role in classifying and categorizing nature into kinds, and that there is no objective fact about nature or its kinds, regardless or independently of our concepts or conceptual schemes.

conceptual truth A **proposition** which is true solely in virtue of the relation between the concepts used in its expression (also called a 'relation of ideas'). For example, the proposition 'triangles have three angles' is a conceptual truth because the concept of a triangle contains the concept of having three angles. Similarly, the proposition 'bachelors are unmarried' is a conceptual truth because the idea of bachelorhood contains the idea of being unmarried. (*See*, by way of contrast, **empirical truth**.)

constructive empiricism An antirealist position (*see* **scientific antirealism**) that denies that our best scientific theories are true. It claims that empirical adequacy (as opposed to truth) is the aim of science (*see* **empirical adequacy**). The view is *empiricist* in claiming that our scientific knowledge should be confined to observable phenomena, those we can see and experience with the naked eye. It acknowledges also the central role of *constructing* scientific models to produce an empirically adequate image of nature.

constructivism This variety of **scientific antirealism** denies that nature (and its objects and entities) exists mind-independently. Instead, scientific objects and entities should be regarded as human constructions. By contrast with conceptual relativists, constructivists tend to stress that our scientific entities and kinds are the products of well-trodden scientific, technological and experimental practices, embedded in well-defined sociocultural contexts.

counterfactual change Change (or impact) which is assessed in terms of the difference that a given event would have made had it *not* occurred. For example, 'If my alarm clock had not gone off this morning, I would have been late for work.'

credulism In contrast to reductionism, credulism is the doctrine that one can be justified in holding a **testimony**-based belief even though one lacks any independent grounds in support of that belief. *See also* **reductionism**.

cultural relativism This is the view that moral statements and judgments are true or false but only relative to the culture in which they are made.

dualism Any view that holds that there are two distinct kinds of thing in some domain can be called dualism. Mind/body dualism is the view that the mind is a different kind of thing from the physical world.

emotivism This is the view that moral statements express emotive attitudes rather than factual beliefs.

empirical adequacy Regarded as a competitor to truth in defining the aim of science. According to constructive empiricists (*see* **constructive empiricism**), science aims to provide us with theories which are *empirically adequate*. And a theory is empirically adequate if what it says about observable things and events in nature is true. Namely, a theory is empirically adequate if it saves the phenomena. *See also* **saving the phenomena**.

empirical judgments These are judgments that can in principle be confirmed by empirical observation, such as the discoveries of science or mundane facts about the world around us. When an empirical judgment is true, it expresses an **empirical truth**.

empirical truth These are **propositions** that are true not in virtue of the relations of the concepts used to express them but in virtue of the way the world is (also called 'matters of fact'). For example, the proposition 'triangles play an important role in the history of Christian art' is an empirical truth. (*See*, by way of contrast, **conceptual truth**.)

Enlightenment, the This was a period of intellectual history, roughly from 1700 to 1800. It was when ideas like reason, science and democracy were on the rise, while ideas like divine rule, religious revelation and tradition were under pressure.

epistemology This is the name given to the theory of knowledge. Those who study epistemology – known as *epistemologists* – are also interested in those notions closely associated with knowledge, such as truth, justification and rationality.

ethics This is one of the main areas of philosophy, concerning what's right/wrong, good/bad, virtuous/vicious, etc.

extended mind hypothesis The claim that parts of the world can be constituents of our mental states. Thus, mental states are not always located just in our head; sometimes they can extend into the world.

external time Time as registered in the world at large – whether by clocks, tidal movements or the spinning of the Earth, etc. Time as registered by the non-time-travelling majority of the universe.

forward time travel Any journey or process which has different durations in **personal time** and **external time** but where personal and external time share the same direction – for example, a journey which has ten minutes personal duration but fifty years external duration.

functionalism The view that we should identify mental states by what they do, rather than by what they are made of. Mental states are caused by sensory perceptions and other mental states, and function to cause behaviours and new mental states.

Gettier cases These are scenarios in which an agent has a justified true belief and yet lacks knowledge because it is substantially due to luck that the belief in question is true. Imagine someone who forms her belief about what the time is by looking at a stopped clock that she has every reason for thinking is working. Crucially, however, she happens to look at the clock at the one time in the day when it is showing the right time, and so forms a true belief as a result. Her belief is thus both true and justified, yet it isn't a case of knowledge, since it is just luck that her belief is true given that the clock is not working. Gettier cases show that the **classical account of knowledge** that analyses knowledge into justified true belief is unsustainable. *See also* **classical account of knowledge**.

Gödel, Kurt (1903–78) Austrian (later American) logician. Published in 1949 a model of Einstein's general theory of relativity for a world which contains **closed timelike curves** through every point in space-time.

grandfather paradox Argument against the logical possibility of **time travel** that assumes that if it is possible to travel in time then it is also possible to create contradictions. For example, if you could travel back in time to before one of your grandfathers became a parent, and assassinated that grandfather, you would thereby prevent yourself from existing and so create a contradiction.

Hume, David (1711–76) David Hume is one of Scotland's most important philosophers, and arguably the greatest ever philosopher to write in the English language. Born in Edinburgh, he led an interesting and varied life, writing a celebrated history of England as well as a number of central works in philosophy. Possibly his greatest work, *A Treatise of Human Nature*, was completed by the time he was 26. Hume's intellectual achievements made him a key figure in a period of history known as **the Enlightenment**, a time of great intellectual ferment.

identity theory The view that mental states are identical with physical states.

immaterial/material substances Material substances occupy a certain amount of space. Immaterial substances do not occupy space.

inference to the best explanation Also known as abductive inference (following C. S. Peirce's terminology), inference to the best explanation is a type of inference or logical reasoning, whereby given two **premises** such as 'if p then q' and 'q', we infer 'p' as the best explanation for 'q'. That is, we infer the hypothesis p that best explains the evidence q (e.g. 'if there is a mouse, the crumbs on the floor will disappear'; 'the crumbs on the floor have disappeared'; and therefore we conclude that 'there is a mouse' as the best explanation for the available evidence).

instrumentalism This is the view that we should regard scientific theories as no more than useful tools to get calculations down, but without any further belief in the truth of the theories.

Kant, Immanuel (1724–1804) Quite possibly the most important and influential philosopher of the modern era. Although he contributed to just about every area of philosophy, he is most known for his transcendental idealism and his contribution to **ethics**. As regards the former, the leading idea was that much of the structure that we ascribe to the world – such as the temporal or causal order – is in fact a product of our minds. In ethics, he is mostly known for arguing that the source of the moral good lies in the good will. A morally good action is thus one that is done with a good will (though note that Kant imposes some rather austere demands on what counts as a good will, so good acts are not as easy to come by as this short precis might suggest!).

Leibniz's law Two things are identical (one and the same) if they share all the same properties.

Lewis, David (1941–2001) American philosopher, specializing in **metaphysics** and **epistemology**. Defended the logical possibility of **time travel** in a celebrated 1976 paper, 'The Paradoxes of Time Travel'.

logical empiricism The name refers to a range of philosophical views defended by members of the so-called Vienna Circle in the early twentieth century (among its exponents, there were Moritz Schlick, Rudolf Carnap, Otto Neurath). Logic and empiricism were regarded as the two main sources for scientific knowledge. Key to the position is the idea that the language of science can be divided into a theoretical vocabulary and an observational vocabulary, where the former should be reducible to the latter.

material substances *see* **immaterial/material substances**

mental state These are states of the mind, often with some content, e.g. having a belief that it is sunny, or the desire to go to the beach. Other examples of mental states include imagining, remembering, hoping and thinking. Sensations are also mental states, e.g. pains, joys, feeling dizzy, although it is less clear what to make of their content. This term is used interchangeably with **psychological states**.

metaethics This is a sub-branch of **ethics**, whose central question is about the **status of morality**.

metaphysics The branch of philosophy which considers questions to do with the nature and structure of reality. Metaphysical topics can include the freedom of the will, personal identity and the nature of space and time.

moral judgments These are judgments concerning ethical questions.

multiply realizable Something is multiply realizable if it can be made from more than one type of material. Chairs, computers, are examples of multiply realizable things.

non-occurrent mental states *see* **occurrent/non-occurrent mental states**

objectivism This is one approach to questions about the **status of morality**; it says that moral statements and judgments can be true or false, and that they are made true or false by objective matters of fact.

occurrent/non-occurrent mental states A mental state is occurrent when you are aware of it, or are thinking about it; a mental state is non-occurrent when you have it but you are not currently aware of it or thinking about it.

personal time This is time as registered by the time traveller or by a time-travelling object. Covers all the processes moving with the time traveller or time-travelling object, so might include time as registered by a time traveller's watch, accumulating memories, or processes of digestion.

philosophy of mind The branch of philosophy broadly concerned with questions of what it is to have a mind. Central questions within the field include how mental phenomena are related to physical phenomena, how we should understand consciousness, whether we have direct access to our own thoughts, and how we come to understand other people's thoughts.

philosophy of science The branch of philosophy that deals with conceptual and foundational issues arising from the sciences. Philosophers of science may tackle general questions about science (e.g. What is the aim of science? What is a law of nature? How does scientific confirmation work? among many others), as well as more specific foundational questions about particular scientific disciplines (in which case, we speak of philosophy of physics, philosophy of biology, philosophy of medicine, philosophy of economics, for example).

physicalism The view that everything which exists can be explained by physics.

premise One of the claims an argument makes in order to support its conclusion.

principle of credulity This principle, due to Thomas Reid, states that human beings are naturally disposed to believe what they are told.

principle of veracity This principle, due to **Thomas Reid**, states that human beings are naturally disposed to speak the truth.

proposition A proposition is what is stated by a declarative sentence. For example, the sentence 'The cat is on the mat' states that something is the case, namely that the cat is on the mat; this is the proposition expressed by this sentence. Notice that the same proposition will be expressed by an analogue declarative sentence in a different language, such as French, just so long as what is stated by that sentence is the same.

propositional knowledge This is knowledge that something (i.e. a **proposition**) is the case. It is typically contrasted with **ability knowledge**, or *know-how*. The two types of knowledge are treated differently because, intuitively at least, one might know how to do something (e.g. swim) without having any relevant propositional knowledge (e.g. without knowing that you can swim, perhaps because you forgot that you could until you fell in the water). *See also* **ability knowledge**.

psychological state *see* **mental state**.

radical scepticism This is the view that we do not know very much, particularly when it comes to our beliefs about the external world (i.e. a world that is 'external' to our experience of it). Although it is natural to speak of radical scepticism as being a philosophical position, it is not usually advanced in this way but is rather put forward as a challenge to existing theories of knowledge to show why they exclude the type of radical scepticism in question.

reductionism In contrast to credulism, reductionism holds that in order for a **testimony**-based belief to be justified, it is essential that the agent concerned is able to offer independent grounds in favour of that belief – that is, grounds which are not themselves further testimony-based beliefs. *See also* **credulism**.

Reid, Thomas (1710–96) Like his contemporary, **David Hume** (1711–76), Thomas Reid was one of the main figures in a period of Scottish intellectual history known as the Scottish Enlightenment, in which radical new ideas came to the fore. Unlike Hume, however, who was notoriously prone to take a sceptical attitude towards the beliefs held by most of those around him, Reid was a defender of what is known as a 'common-sense' philosophy, which put the claims of common sense above the conclusions of abstract philosophical reasoning.

relativism This is one approach to questions about the **status of morality**; it says that moral statements and judgments can be true or false but only relative to something that can vary across different people.

replacement change Change (or impact) in which an object (or state of affairs) is replaced by another object (or state of affairs). For example, if I break my mug, I replace an intact mug with a mass of mug fragments. Likewise, when an armistice is declared a state of peace replaces a state of war.

saving the phenomena The expression comes from the ancient Greek and has been translated literally as such in English. In the context of the debate between realism and antirealism in science, the expression means to account for the phenomena, or to accommodate the phenomena, i.e. to be able to provide an accurate analysis of them without having to introduce unnecessary beliefs in unobservable entities. *See also* **empirical adequacy**.

sceptical hypotheses A sceptical hypothesis is a scenario in which you are radically deceived about the world and yet your experience of the world is exactly as it would be had you not been deceived. The problem posed by sceptical hypotheses is that we seem unable to know that they are false. Accordingly, how could we ever hope to distinguish a genuine experience of the world from an illusory one? Sceptical hypotheses are thus used to motivate scepticism. *See also* **radical scepticism**.

scientific antirealism The opposite of realism, it comes in many flavours, depending on which aspect of realism one may want to play down (*see also* **scientific realism**). Thus, an antirealist can, for example: (a) deny that nature (and its objects and entities) exist mind-independently; or (b) deny that our best scientific theories are true; or (c) deny that scientific language refers to or picks out objects in nature. (a) includes **conceptual relativism** and **constructivism**. (b) includes **constructive empiricism**. (c) is known as semantic antirealism.

scientific realism The view that science aims to give us a literally true story about nature. A scientific realist typically endorses the following three claims: (a) that nature (and its objects and entities) exist mind-independently (metaphysical aspect); (b) that our best scientific theories are true, i.e. what they say about nature and its objects corresponds to the way nature is (epistemic aspect); (c) that scientific language refers to or picks out objects existing mind-independently in nature (semantic aspect). Typically a realist sees science as progressing towards better and better theories, which are closer to the truth (or approximately true).

semantic *see* **syntax/semantics**

sound An argument is sound when it is **valid** with true **premises**.

status of morality This is the central issue of **metaethics**. It is about whether moral statements and judgments can be true or false, and if they can, whether they are made true or false by objective matters of fact or facts that are somehow relative.

subjectivism This is the view that moral statements and judgments are true or false but only relative to the subjective perspective of the particular individual who makes them.

syntactic *see* **syntax/semantics**

syntax/semantics Syntax and semantics are properties of *symbols*. The semantic property of a symbol is what it stands for. The syntactic properties of a symbol are its geometric and internal properties. Syntax also refers to the rules that govern how these geometric and internal features can be changed and combined.

testimony Philosophers understand the notion of testimony quite broadly to include not just the formal verbal transmission of information that one finds taking place in, say, a courtroom, but also the intentional transmission of information in general – whether verbally or through books, pictures, videos, and so on.

time travel Any journey or process which has different durations in **personal time** and **external time**.

valid An argument is valid when the truth of its conclusion follows from the truth of its **premises**. That is, if the premises are all true, then there is no way the conclusion could be false.

Bibliography

Adler, J. (2012) 'Epistemological Problems of Testimony', in E. Zalta (ed.) *Stanford Encyclopedia of Philosophy* [online encyclopedia], http://plato. stanford.edu/entries/testimony-episprob/ (accessed 23 May 2013).

Arntzenius, F. and Maudlin, T. (2005) 'Time Travel and Modern Physics', in E. Zalta (ed.) *Stanford Encyclopedia of Philosophy* [online encyclopedia] (Summer 2005 edn), http://plato.stanford.edu/archives/sum2005/entries/time-travel-phys/ (accessed 23 May 2013).

Berlin, I. (1980) 'The Purpose of Philosophy', in his *Concepts and Categories: Philosophical Essays*, Oxford: Oxford University Press.

Blackburn, S. (1999) *Think*, New York: Oxford University Press.

——(2002) *Being Good: A Short Introduction to Ethics*, Oxford: Oxford University Press.

Blackmore, S. (2005) *Conversations on Consciousness*, Oxford: Oxford University Press.

Buchan, J. (2003) *Capital of the Mind: How Edinburgh Changed the World*, Edinburgh: Birlinn.

Chakravartty, A. (2011) 'Scientific Realism', in E. Zalta (ed.) *Stanford Encyclopedia of Philosophy* [online encyclopedia], http://plato.stanford.edu/entries/scientific-realism/(accessed 29 May 2013).

Chrisman, M. (2011) 'Ethical Expressivism', in C. Miller (ed.) *The Continuum Companion to Ethics*, London: Continuum.

——(2013) 'Emotivism', in H. Lafollette (ed.) *International Encyclopedia of Ethics*. Chichester: Wiley-Blackwell.

Churchland, P. and Hooker, C. A. (eds) (1985) *Images of Science*, Chicago: University of Chicago Press.

Clark, A. (2008) *Supersizing the Mind*, Oxford: Oxford University Press.

Clark, A. and Chalmers, D. (1998) 'The Extended Mind', *Analysis* 58: 7–19.

Coady, C. A. J. (1992) *Testimony: A Philosophical Study*, Oxford: Clarendon Press.

Coady, D. (2012) *What to Believe Now: Applying Epistemology to Contemporary Issues*, Chichester: Wiley-Blackwell.

Crane, T. (1995) *The Mechanical Mind*, London: Penguin.

Dainton, B. (2010) *Time and Space*, 2nd edn, Durham: Acumen.

Descartes, R. (1641/1996) *Meditations on First Philosophy*, trans. J. Cottingham, with an introduction by B. Williams, Cambridge: Cambridge University Press.

Deutsch, D. (1997) *The Fabric of Reality*, London: Penguin.

Dowe, P. (2000) 'The Case for Time Travel', *Philosophy* 75: 441–51.

Duhem, P. (1908/1969) *To Save the Phenomena: An Essay on the Idea of Physical Theory from Plato to Galileo*, trans. E. Dolan, Chicago: University of Chicago Press.

Dwyer, L. (1975) 'Time Travel and Changing the Past', *Philosophical Studies* 27: 341–50.

Earman, J. and Wüthrich, C. (2004) 'Time Machines', in E. Zalta (ed.) *Stanford Encyclopedia of Philosophy* (Fall 2008 edn) [online encyclopedia], http://plato.stanford.edu/archives/fall2008/entries/time-machine/ (accessed 23 May 2013).

Fogelin, R. J. (2003) *A Defense of Hume on Miracles*, Princeton, NJ: Princeton University Press.

Frigg, R. and Hartmann, S. (2012) 'Models in Science', in E. Zalta (ed.) *Stanford Encyclopedia of Philosophy* [online encyclopedia], http://plato.stanford.edu/entries/models-science/ (accessed 10 May 2013).

Gettier, E. (1963) 'Is Justified True Belief Knowledge?', *Analysis* 23: 121–23.

Gödel, K. (1949) 'An Example of a New Type of Cosmological Solutions of Einstein's Field Equations of Gravitation', *Reviews of Modern Physics* 21: 447–50.

Gowans, C. (2008) 'Moral Relativism', in E. Zalta (ed.) *Stanford Encyclopedia of Philosophy* [online encyclopedia], (Spring 2012 edn), http://plato.stanford.edu/entries/moral-relativism/ (accessed 13 May 2013).

Greco, J. (2007) 'External World Skepticism', *Philosophy Compass* 2, no 4: 624–95.

Green, C. (2008) 'Epistemology of Testimony', in B. Dowden and J. Fieser (eds) *Internet Encyclopedia of Philosophy* [online encyclopedia], www.iep.utm.edu/e/ep-testi.htm (accessed 29 May 2013).

Grey, W. (1999) 'Troubles with Time Travel', *Philosophy* 74: 55–70.

Harman, G. and Thomson, J. J. (1996) *Moral Relativism and Moral Objectivity*, Malden, MA: Blackwell.

Hawking, S. (1999) 'Space and Time Warps', *Stephen Hawking* [website], www.hawking.org.uk/space-and-time-warps.html (accessed 23 May 2013).

Hetherington, S. (2005) 'Gettier Problems', in B. Dowden and J. Fieser (eds) *Internet Encyclopedia of Philosophy* [online encyclopedia], www.iep.utm.edu/g/gettier.htm (accessed 29 May 2013).

——(2010) 'The Gettier Problem', chapter 12 of S. Bernecker and D. H. Pritchard (eds) *The Routledge Companion to Epistemology*, London: Routledge.

Hofstadter, D. and Dennett, D. D. (eds) (1981) *The Mind's I: Fantasies and Reflections on Self and Soul*, New York: Basic Books.

Horwich, P. (1975) 'On Some Alleged Paradoxes of Time Travel', *Journal of Philosophy* 72: 432–44.

Hume, D. (1739/1978) *A Treatise of Human Nature*, ed. L. A. Selby-Bigge and P. H. Nidditch, 2nd edn, Oxford: Oxford University Press, 1978.

——(1748/1975) *Enquiry Concerning Human Understanding*, in *Enquiries Concerning Human Understanding and Concerning the Principles of Morals*, ed. L. A. Selby-Bigge, 3rd edn, Oxford: Oxford University Press.

——(1777/1993) *Dialogues Concerning Natural Religion* and *The Natural History of Religion*, ed. J. C. A. Gaskin, Oxford: Oxford University Press, 1993.

Ichikawa, J. and Steup, M. (2012) 'The Analysis of Knowledge', in E. Zalta (ed.) *Stanford Encyclopedia of Philosophy* [online encyclopedia], http://plato.stanford.edu/entries/knowledge-analysis/ (accessed 29 May 2013).

Joll, N. (2010) 'Contemporary Metaphilosophy', in B. Dowden and J. Fieser (eds) *Internet Encyclopedia of Philosophy* [online encyclopedia], www.iep.utm.edu/con-meta/ (accessed 30 May 2013).

Kant, I. (1784/1991) 'An Answer to the Question: "What Is Enlightenment?"', trans. H. B. Nisbet, in *Kant: Political Writings*, ed. H. Reiss, Cambridge: Cambridge University Press.

——(1787/1998) *Critique of Pure Reason*, trans. P. Guyer and A. Wood, New York: Cambridge University Press.

Kim, J. (2006) *The Philosophy of Mind*, Boulder, CO: Westview.

Kitcher, P. (1993) *The Advancement of Science*, New York: Oxford University Press.

Klein, P. (2010) 'Skepticism', in E. Zalta (ed.) *Stanford Encyclopedia of Philosophy* [online encyclopedia], http://plato.stanford.edu/entries/skepticism/ (accessed 23 May 2013).

Lackey, J. (2011) 'Testimonial Knowledge', chapter 29 of S. Bernecker and D. H. Pritchard (eds) *The Routledge Companion to Epistemology*, London: Routledge.

Ladyman, J. (2002) *Understanding Philosophy of Science*, New York: Routledge.

LaFollette, H. (ed.) (2013) *International Encyclopedia of Ethics*, Chichester: Wiley-Blackwell, http://onlinelibrary.wiley.com/book/10.1002/9781444367072 (accessed 23 May 2013).

Lewis, David (1976) 'The Paradoxes of Time Travel', *American Philosophical Quarterly* 13: 145–52.

Lipton, P. (2004) *Inference to the Best Explanation*, 2nd edn, London: Routledge.

Luper, S. (2010) 'Cartesian Skepticism', in S. Bernecker and D. H. Pritchard (eds) *The Routledge Companion to Epistemology*, London: Routledge.

Mackie, J. L. (1977) *Ethics: Inventing Right and Wrong*, London: Penguin.

Miller, A. (2013) *An Introduction to Contemporary Metaethics*, Cambridge: Polity.

Miller, K. (2006) 'Travelling in Time: How to Wholly Exist in Two Places at the Same Time', *Canadian Journal of Philosophy* 36: 309–34.

Monton, B. (ed.) (2007) *Images of Empiricism*, New York: Oxford University Press.

Monton, B. and Mohler, C. (2012) 'Constructive Empiricism', in E. Zalta (ed.) *Stanford Encyclopedia of Philosophy* [online encyclopedia], http://plato.stanford.edu/entries/constructive-empiricism/ (accessed 10 May 2013).

Morgan, M. and Morrison, M. (1999) *Models as Mediators*, Cambridge: Cambridge University Press.

Morris, W. E. (2009) 'Hume', in E. Zalta (ed.) *Stanford Encyclopedia of Philosophy* [online encyclopedia] http://plato.stanford.edu/entries/hume/. (accessed 29 May 2013).

Murdoch, I. (1970) *The Sovereignty of Good*, Bristol: Routledge & Kegan Paul.

Nagel, T. (1974) 'What Is It Like to Be a Bat', *Philosophical Review* 83, no. 4: 435–50.

——(1989) *What Does It All Mean?*, New York: Oxford University Press.

Nahin, P. (1999) *Time Machines: Time Travel in Physics, Metaphysics and Science Fiction*, 2nd edn, New York: American Institute of Physics.

Prinz, J. J. (2007) *The Emotional Construction of Morals*, New York: Oxford University Press.

Pritchard, D. (2009) *Knowledge*, Basingstoke: Palgrave Macmillan.

——(2013) *What Is This Thing Called Knowledge?*, 3rd edn, London: Routledge.

Pritchard, D. and Richmond, A. (2012) 'Hume on Miracles', in A. Bailey and D. O'Brien (eds) *The Continuum Companion to Hume*, London: Continuum, pp. 227–44.

Psillos, S. (1999) *Scientific Realism: How Science Tracks Truth*, London: Routledge.

Putnam, H. (1967) 'The Nature of Mental States', in *Mind, Language and Reality: Philosophical Papers*, vol. 2, Cambridge: Cambridge University Press, pp. 429–40.

——(1978) 'What Is Realism?', in *Meaning and the Moral Sciences*, London: Routledge.

Reid, T. (1764/1997) *An Inquiry into the Human Mind on the Principles of Common Sense*, ed. D. R. Brookes, Edinburgh: Edinburgh University Press.

Richmond, A. (2001) 'Time-Travel Fictions and Philosophy', *American Philosophical Quarterly* 38: 305–18.

——(2003) 'Recent Work: Time Travel', *Philosophical Books* 44: 297–309.

Rosenberg, J. (1996) *The Practice of Philosophy: A Handbook for Beginners*, Upper Saddle River, NJ: Prentice Hall.

Russell, B. (1998) *The Problems of Philosophy*, Oxford: Oxford University Press.

Sayre-McCord, G. (2012) 'Metaethics', in E. Zalta (ed.) *Stanford Encyclopedia of Philosophy* [online encyclopedia], http://plato.stanford.edu/entries/metaethics/ (accessed 23 May 2013).

Schroeder, M. (2010) *Noncognitivism in Ethics*, New York: Routledge.

Schwarz, P. (n.d.) *Time Travel in Flatland: An Animated Tutorial in Physics, Light Cones and Causality*, California Institute of Technology [website], www.theory.caltech.edu/people/patricia/lctoc.html (accessed 23 May 2013).

Searle, J. (1980) 'Minds, Brains and Programs', *Behavioral and Brain Sciences* 3: 417–24.

——(1998) *The Mystery of Consciousness*, New York: New York Review of Books.

Sellars, W. (1962) 'Philosophy and the Scientific Image of Man', in R. Colodny (ed.) *Frontiers of Science and Philosophy*, Pittsburgh, PA: University of Pittsburgh Press.

Shafer-Landau, R. (2004) *Whatever Happened to Good and Evil?*, New York: Oxford University Press.

Shope, R. (2002) 'Conditions and Analyses of Knowing', in P. K. Moser (ed.) *The Oxford Handbook of Epistemology*, Oxford: Oxford University Press, pp. 25–70.

Smith, M. (1994) *The Moral Problem*, Oxford: Blackwell.

Smith, N. J. J. (1997) 'Bananas Enough for Time Travel?', *British Journal for the Philosophy of Science* 48: 363–89.

Smith, P. and Jones, O. R. (1986) *The Philosophy of Mind*, Cambridge: Cambridge University Press.

Sorensen, R. (1987) 'Time Travel, Parahistory and Hume', *Philosophy* 62: 227–36.

Steup, M., Turri, J. and Sosa, E. (eds) (2013) *Contemporary Debates in Epistemology*, 2nd edn, Oxford: Blackwell.

Strawson, P. F. (1962) 'Freedom and Resentment', *Proceedings of the British Academy* 48: 1–25.

Turing, A. (1950) 'Computing Machinery and Intelligence', *Mind* 59: 433–60.

van Fraassen, B. (1980) *The Scientific Image*, Oxford: Clarendon.

Vihvelin, K. (1996) 'What Time Travelers Cannot Do', *Philosophical Studies* 81: 315–30.

Williams, B. A. O. (1985) *Ethics and the Limits of Philosophy*, Cambridge, MA: Harvard University Press.

Yaffe, G. and Nichols, R. (2009), 'Reid', in E. Zalta (ed.) *Stanford Encyclopedia of Philosophy* [online encyclopedia] http://plato.stanford.edu/entries/reid/. (accessed 29 May 2013).

Yourgrau, P. (1999) *Gödel Meets Einstein*, Chicago: Open Court.

Zagzebski, L. (1999) 'What Is Knowledge?' in J. Greco and E. Sosa (eds) *The Blackwell Companion to Epistemology*, Oxford: Blackwell, pp. 92–116.

Index

Page numbers in italics indicate figures.

American Philosophy in *The Basics*

American Philosophy: The Basics

Nancy Stanlick, University of Central Florida

American Philosophy: The Basics introduces the history of American thought from early Calvinists to the New England Transcendentalists and from contract theory to contemporary African American philosophy. The key question it asks is: what it is that makes American Philosophy unique? This lively and compelling book moves through key periods in the development of American thought from the founding fathers to the transcendentalists and pragmatists to contemporary social commentators. Readers are introduced to:

- Some of the most important thinkers in American history including Jonathan Edwards, Thomas Paine, Charles Sanders Pierce, Thomas Kuhn, Cornel West and many more

- Developments in five key areas of thought: epistemology, metaphysics, religion and ethics, social philosophy, and political philosophy

- The contributions of American women, African-Americans and Native Americans.

Featuring suggestions for further reading and assuming no prior knowledge of philosophy, this is an ideal first introduction for anyone studying or interested in the history of American thought.

November 2012 – 180 pages
Pb: 978-0-415-68970-0| Hb: 978-0-415-68972-4

For more information and to order a copy visit
http://www.routledge.com/books/details/9780415689700/

Available from all good bookshops